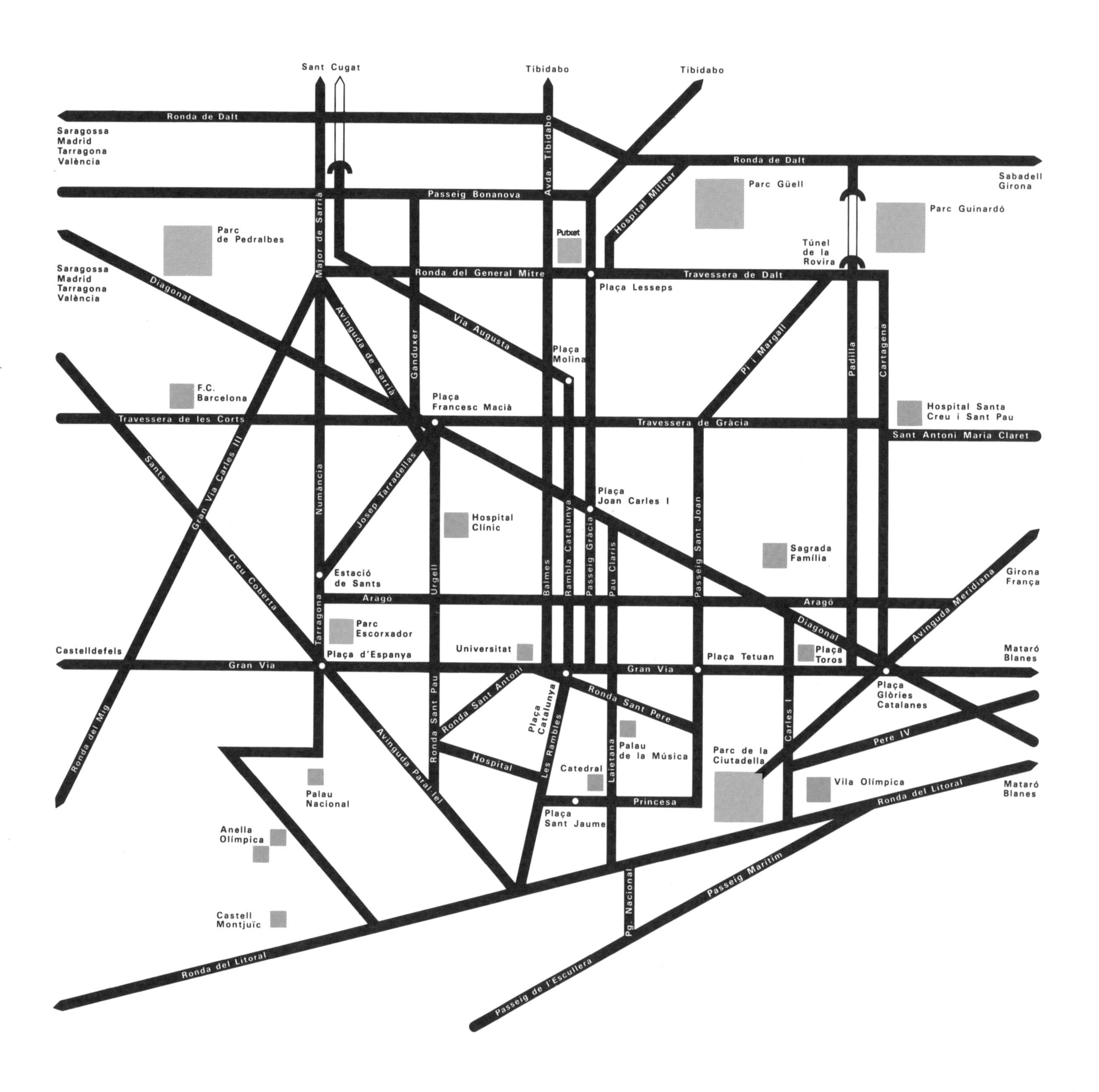

Sant Cugat
Tibidabo
Tibidabo
Ronda de Dalt
Saragossa
Madrid
Tarragona
València
Ronda de Dalt
Sabadell
Girona
Passeig Bonanova
Avda. Tibidabo
Hospital Militar
Parc Güell
Parc Guinardó
Parc
de Pedralbes
Putxet
Túnel
de la
Rovira
Saragossa
Madrid
Tarragona
València
Major de Sarrià
Ronda del General Mitre
Travessera de Dalt
Plaça Lesseps
Diagonal
Avinguda de Sarrià
Ganduxer
Via Augusta
Plaça
Molina
Pi i Margall
Padilla
Cartagena
F.C.
Barcelona
Plaça
Francesc Macià
Hospital Santa
Creu i Sant Pau
Travessera de les Corts
Travessera de Gràcia
Sant Antoni Maria Claret
Sants
Gran Via Carles III
Numància
Josep Tarradellas
Plaça
Joan Carles I
Hospital
Clínic
Passeig Sant Joan
Sagrada
Família
Creu Coberta
Estació
de Sants
Urgell
Balmes
Rambla Catalunya
Passeig Gràcia
Pau Claris
Girona
França
Aragó
Aragó
Avinguda Meridiana
Parc
Escorxador
Tarragona
Diagonal
Castelldefels
Plaça d'Espanya
Universitat
Plaça Tetuan
Plaça
Toros
Mataró
Blanes
Gran Via
Gran Via
Ronda Sant Antoni
Ronda Sant Pere
Plaça
Glòries
Catalanes
Ronda del Mig
Avinguda Paral·lel
Ronda Sant Pau
Plaça
Catalunya
Palau
de la Música
Parc de la
Ciutadella
Carles I
Pere IV
Hospital
Les Rambles
Catedral
Laietana
Vila Olímpica
Mataró
Blanes
Palau
Nacional
Plaça
Sant Jaume
Princesa
Ronda del Litoral
Anella
Olímpica
Pg. Nacional
Passeig Marítim
Castell
Montjuïc
Ronda del Litoral
Passeig de l'Escullera

Barcelona

Barcelona

Fotografías / Photographs / Fotografien
Pere Vivas – Ricard Pla

Edición / Published by / Verlag
Triangle Postals

2 Detalle del banco del Park Güell
Detail of the bench in Park Güell
Nahaufnahme der Bank im Park Güell

3 El Port Olímpic desde la Escollera
The Port Olímpic from the breakwater
Blick von der Mole auf den Port Olímpic

4 Pasarela del Port Vell
Port Vell Footbridge
Fußgängerbrücke im Port Vell

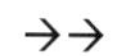

5 Rambla de les Flors
Rambla de les Flors
Rambla de les Flors

MAREMAGNUM

LA VANGUARDIA
BANCA CATALANA

Comercial
Montolio y
Morenete s.l.
suministros
para
relojeria
CONSULTORI · MÈDIC
9 - La Flor de la Rambla

VASCO

Barcelona

Contemplada desde la montaña del Tibidabo, Barcelona nos muestra un denso entramado de calles dispuestas sobre la llanura extendida frente al mar, entre los ríos Llobregat y Besòs, y protegida por la sierra de Collserola. La historia y el azar determinaron este tejido urbano que alterna espacios caprichosos y entreverados con otros más rectilíneos y racionales. El horizonte marino que desde aquí alcanzamos se funde con la historia mediterránea de esta ciudad de luz cálida, heredera de culturas diversas. De sus orígenes ibéricos, el contacto con el mundo griego y la refundación romana como colonia Barcino, Barcelona pasó a ejercer la capitalidad de Cataluña desde el siglo X.

El corazón de la ciudad se corresponde con el antiguo perímetro amurallado de la época romana —cuyo trazado, de sobria y robusta factura, aún podemos seguir hoy con fidelidad— y las posteriores ampliaciones medievales, espacio dulcificado por el río de vida de la Rambla y el límite marítimo del puerto. Durante siglos, la expansión comercial de los barceloneses por el Mediterráneo favoreció el desarrollo económico, potenció los gremios de artesanos y la industria relacionada con la navegación. El edificio de la Llotja, la iglesia de Santa María del Mar y Les Drassanes nos hablan, desde la excepción de su arquitectura única, de aquellos momentos de esplendor, al igual que la historia y los nombres de muchas calles y plazas.

El peculiar trazado de esta parte de la ciudad permite redescubrir constantemente numerosos rincones y detalles de interés, calles estrechas y esquivas al sol dan lugar a otros espacios de rara belleza con edificios de valiosa arquitectura, restaurados y habilitados ahora para nuevo uso público. Desde la fundación romana, los órganos de gobierno se situaron en el centro de este barrio his-

←←

6 Anochecer en la terraza de "La Pedrera"
Nightfall on the terrace of "La Pedrera"
Abenddämmerung auf der Terrasse der „Pedrera"

tórico —aquí tuvo su sede el primer parlamento democrático de Europa, el Consell de Cent—, y hoy encontramos, frente a frente, las sedes de las máximas representaciones ciudadanas, la Casa de la Ciutat y la Generalitat de Catalunya.

Durante siglos la vida de los barceloneses transcurrió en este perímetro exiguo, hasta que la necesidad de crecimiento aconsejó el ensanche de la ciudad. El derribo de las murallas que ahogaban la Barcelona antigua coincidió con el crecimiento económico y el desarrollo industrial, cuyo impulso generará riqueza y buena arquitectura. Se inicia así una nueva era para la ciudad y la oportunidad de contar por primera vez con soluciones urbanísticas como punto de partida.

La planificación que permitió el ensanche de Barcelona fue ideada por Ildefons Cerdà, a mediados del siglo XIX, con la intención de racionalizar el espacio comprendido entre la ciudad vieja y las poblaciones próximas que quedarían absorbidas por el crecimiento. La transformación efectuada en Barcelona a lo largo de medio siglo, contrapunto del carácter denso y, a veces, anárquico de la ciudad, no encuentra comparación en Europa. La peculiar "cuadrícula" del Eixample, resultado final de la expansión, forma un tejido urbano uniforme, alterado por las construcciones modernistas más atrevidas. El modernismo fue aquí la expresión de un deseo, el de situar la cultura catalana a la altura de las más importantes de Europa; una cultura que fuera expresión de la potencia económica del país y de los anhelos de libertad y modernidad.

Dos acontecimientos importantes enmarcan el crecimiento de la ciudad y simbolizan la recuperación de nuevos espacios: la Exposición Universal de 1888 y la Exposición Internacional de 1929.

En la primera, los arquitectos modernistas iniciaban su andadura; en la segunda, la arquitectura racionalista ya mostraba sus primeras manifestaciones. Entre estas dos fechas, numerosos artistas —Domènech i Montaner, Gaudí, Puig i Cadafalch, Picasso, Gargallo, Miró, etc.—, favorecidos por los aires renovadores que vivía la ciudad, completaban o iniciaban su obra, producto de una época excepcional, tan rica en nuevas propuestas culturales como esperanzadora y utópica en sus ansias de transformación social.

La Barcelona que disfrutamos hoy es la suma de todos estos periodos, de los que el tiempo ha dejado una huella generosa. Pero en estos últimos años una nueva Barcelona ha emergido, fruto de la gran transformación urbanística que se inició con la cita olímpica de 1992 y que tuvo su continuidad en los años posteriores, en los que han dejado su huella los mejores arquitectos y artistas internacionales. Es la Barcelona renovada y moderna que se ha convertido en uno de los destinos turísticos preferidos en el mundo.

Nuestro libro pretende reflejar con fidelidad la imagen global de esta Barcelona vivida y sentida, capaz de devolvernos con sus imágenes los escenarios del recuerdo.

Borja Calzado

7 Porta de la Pau

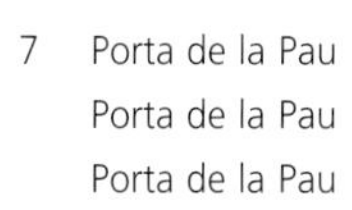

Porta de la Pau

Porta de la Pau

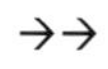

8 Interior del Estadio Olímpico

Interior of the Olympic Stadium

Olympiastadium von innen

Jeux de la XXVe Olympiade
Games of the XXV Olympiad

Barcelona

Seen from the mountain top of Tibidabo, Barcelona shows us a dense network of streets arranged across the plain facing the sea, between the Llobregat and Besòs rivers, and sheltered by the Collserola range. History and chance have shaped this urban fabric which alternates between fanciful and mixed up spaces with other straighter and more rational ones. The horizon of the sea, which we can see from here, merges with the Mediterranean history of this city of warm light, the heir to diverse cultures. From its Iberian origins, the contact with the Greek world and the Roman refoundation as the Barcino colony, Barcelona has been the capital city of Catalonia since the 10th century.

The heart of the city corresponds to the old walled perimeter of the Roman era — whose design, simply and solidly made, can be clearly traced today — and the later medieval extensions, a space freshened by the river of life of the Rambla and the sea limits of the port. For centuries, the expansion in trade carried out by the citizens of Barcelona favoured economic development and strengthened the craftsmen's guilds and the industry related to navigation. The building of the Llotja, the church of Santa Maria del Mar and the Drassanes tells us, from the singularity of their unique architecture, of those times of splendour, as do the history and names of many streets and squares.

The unusual layout of this part of the city enables one to continuously rediscover many little corners and interesting details, and narrow streets, hidden from the sun, lead to other spaces of rare beauty with buildings of valuable architecture, today restored and fitted up for new public use. From Roman times the governing bodies have been located in the heart of this historic district — the Consell de Cent, the Council of one hundred, the first democratic parliament in Europe, had its headquarters here — and today we find, facing each other, the headquarters of the main public authorities, that of the City Council and of the autonomous government, the Generalitat de Catalunya.

For centuries the lives of Barcelona's inhabitants took place within this minuscule perimeter, until the need for growth required the city to expand. The demolition of the walls that were choking the old Barcelona coincided with economic growth and industrial development, whose impetus created wealth and fine architecture. Thus a new era began for the city and the opportunity, for the first time, to propose urban planning solutions as a starting point.

The planning for the enlargement of Barcelona was the brainwave of Ildefons Cerdà, in the mid-19th century, with the aim of rationalising the space between the old city and the outlying villages that were being absorbed by growth. The transformation carried out in Barcelona during half a century, in contrast with the dense and sometimes anarchic character of the city, was unequalled in all Europe. The special "grid" of the Eixample, the end result of the expansion, forms a uniform urban fabric, broken up by the most daring modernist constructions. Modernism here was an expression of a desire to place Catalan culture on a level with the most important cultures in Europe: a culture that was the expression of the country's economic power and of the yearning for freedom and modernity.

Two important events mark the city's growth and symbolise the recovery of new spaces: the Universal Exhibition of 1888 and the International Exhibition of 1929. In the former, the modernist architects began their professional careers and by the time of the latter, rationalist architecture had already begun to express itself. Between these two dates, many artists — Domènech i Montaner, Gaudí, Puig i Cadafalch, Picasso, Gargallo, Miró, etc. — aided by the airs of renewal that the city experienced, finished or began their work, the result of an exceptional period, as rich in new cultural approaches as it was hopeful and utopian in its longing for social change.

The Barcelona we enjoy today is the sum of all these periods, of which time has left a deep and generous mark. In recent years, however, a new Barcelona has emerged, the result of the massive urban transformation that begun with the Olympic Games in 1992 and continued in the following years, in which the top international architects and artists have left their mark. It is the renewed and modern Barcelona that has become one of the world's leading tourist destinations.

Our book aims to faithfully reflect the overall image of this enjoyed and felt Barcelona, with images that take us back to the settings of those memorable times.

Borja Calzado

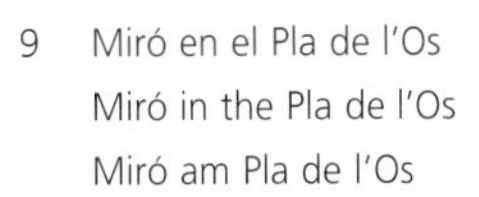

9 Miró en el Pla de l'Os
Miró in the Pla de l'Os
Miró am Pla de l'Os

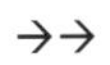

10 Palau de la Música Catalana
Palau de la Música Catalana
Palau de la Música Catalana

VILA

Barcelona

Wenn wir die Stadt von dem Berg Tibidabo aus betrachten, liegt das dichte Straßengeflecht von Barcelona auf einer Ebene, die sich zum Meer hin öffnet. Begrenzt wird die Stadt von den Flüssen Llobregat und Besòs, und beschützt von der Gebirgskette Sierra de Collserola. Die urbane Struktur wurde von der Geschichte und von Zufällen geprägt, ausgefallene und allmählich gewachsene Flächen wechseln sich mit geraden und rationalen Linien ab. Der Meereshorizont, den wir von hier aus sehen, verschmilzt mit der mediterranen Geschichte dieser vom warmen Licht geprägten Stadt, Erbin verschiedener Kulturen. Ihre Ursprünge sind auf die Iberer zurückzuführen, dann war sie mit der Welt der Griechen in Berührung und wurde von den Römern als die Kolonie Barcino neu gegründet, bis Barcelona schließlich ab dem X. Jahrhundert zur Hauptstadt Kataloniens wurde.

Die Stadtmitte aus der romanischen Epoche, die einst von einer Stadtmauer umgeben wurde, ist das Herz Barcelonas. Wir können auch heute noch den genauen Verlauf der schlichten und robusten Stadtmauer verfolgen. Im Mittelalter fanden dann die ersten Stadterweiterungen statt; es entstanden neue, vom Hafen und vom Meer begrenzte Viertel, die durch das lebendige Treiben auf den Rambles an Nüchternheit verloren. Jahrhundertelang wurde die wirtschaftliche Entwicklung durch den Handel am Mittelmeer begünstigt, es entstanden mächtige Handwerkszünfte und der Schiffbau entwickelte sich zu einem bedeutenden Wirtschaftszweig. Die ehemalige Börse La Llotja, die Kirche Santa Maria del Mar und Les Drassanes lassen uns in ihrer architektonischen Schönheit jene glanzvollen Momente erkennen, an die auch die Geschichte der Stadt und die Namen vieler Straßen und Plätze erinnern.

Der eigentümliche Straßenverlauf in der Altsladt läßt uns ständig Ecken und interessante Einzelheiten wieder entdecken. Enge und schattige Gassen führen zu einzigartig schönen Plätzen mit architektonisch sehr wertvollen Gebäuden, die renoviert und zu öffentlichen Gebäuden umgebaut wurden. Seit der Stadtgründung in der Zeit der Römer befanden sich die Regierungsorgane im Zentrum der Altstadt, und hier befand sich auch der Sitz des ersten, demokratischen Parlamentes Europas, des Consell de Cent. Auch heute befinden sich dort einander gegenüber die beiden höchsten Bürgervertretungen, das Rathaus Casa de la Ciutat und die Landesregierung, die Generalitat de Catalunya.

Jahrhundertelang fand das Leben der Einwohner Barcelonas auf diesem so engen Raum statt, bis dieser Platzmangel zur Stadterweiterung führte. Der Abriss der Stadtmauern, welche das alte Barcelona erdrückten, fand in der Zeit des wirtschaftlichen Wachstums und der industriellen Entwicklung statt, durch die Reichtum und prächtige Architektur gefördert wurden. So begann eine neue Ära für die Stadt, denn zum ersten Mal bildeten urbanistische Lösungsvorschläge einen neuen Ausgangspunkt.

Die Pläne, welche die Erweiterung der Stadt ermöglichten, wurden Mitte des XIX. Jahrhunderts von Ildefons Cerdà geschaffen. Absicht des Erweiterungsplanes war es, den Raum zwischen der Altstadt und den nahe gelegenen Orten, welche durch das Wachstum integriert wurden, rational aufzuteilen. Diese Umformung, die in Barcelona ein halbes Jahrhundert lang stattfand und durch die ein Kontrast zu der dichtbesiedelten und manchmal anarchischen Altstadt entstand, fand so nirgendwo sonst in Europa statt. Die eigentümliche, quadratische Struktur des Viertels Eixample, Ergebnis dieser Stadterweiterung, bildet ein gleichförmiges, urbanes Muster, das durch die gewagtesten, modernistischen Gebäude unterbrochen wird. Der Modernismus war in dieser Stadt Ausdruck eines Wunsches, nämlich des Wunsches, die katalanische Kultur auf die Höhe der wichtigsten Kulturströmungen Europas zu bringen. Diese katalanische Kultur war auch der Ausdruck der Wirtschaftsmacht des Landes und der Sehnsucht nach Freiheit und Modernität.

Zwei wichtige Ereignisse umrahmen das Wachstum der Stadt und stellen ein Symbol für die Eroberung neuer, städtischer Räume dar, die Weltausstellung 1888 und die Internationale Ausstellung 1929. Mit der Weltausstellung begannen die ersten modernistischen Architekten ihre Arbeit, in der zweiten Ausstellung manifestierte sich schon die rationalistische Architektur. Zwischen diesen beiden Daten begannen oder beendeten, begünstigt durch den die Stadt beherrschenden Wunsch nach Erneuerung, zahlreiche Künstler wie Domènech i Muntaner, Gaudí, Puig i Cadafalch, Picasso, Gargallo, Miró etc., ihre Werke, Produkte einer ganz besonderen Epoche voller neuer, kultureller Vorschläge und vielversprechender und utopischer Bemühungen um die soziale Umformung.

Das Barcelona, das wir heute genießen können, ist das Ergebnis all jener Epochen, deren Erbe sich bis in die heutige Zeit erhalten hat. Aber in den letzten Jahren ist ein neues Barcelona entstanden, bedingt durch die umgreifenden, urbanen Veränderungen, die mit der Olympiade im Jahr 1992 begannen und in den nachfolgenden Jahren fortgesetzt wurden, und an denen die besten internationalen Architekten und Künstler beteiligt sind. Das ist das neue und moderne Barcelona, heute eines der beliebtesten Reiseziele der Welt.

In unserem Buch möchten wir ein treues, globales Bild dieses gelebten und gefühlten Barcelonas geben, und durch die Bilder die Erinnerung an die erlebten Orte zurückbringen.

Borja Calzado

↑

11 "Casa de les Punxes"
"Casa de les Punxes"
„Casa de les Punxes"

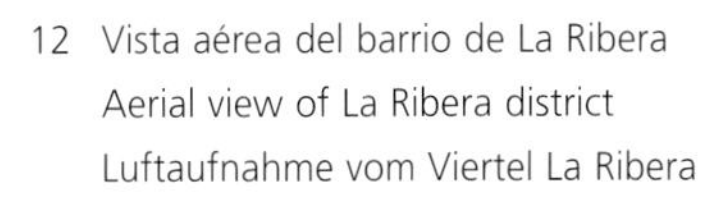

12 Vista aérea del barrio de La Ribera
Aerial view of La Ribera district
Luftaufnahme vom Viertel La Ribera

13 Museu d'Art Contemporani de Barcelona
The Museum of Modern Art of Barcelona
Museu d'Art Contemporani de Barcelona

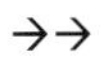

14 Visión nocturna del Port Vell
Night view of Port Vell
Nächtlicher Blick auf den Port Vell

MAREMAGNUM

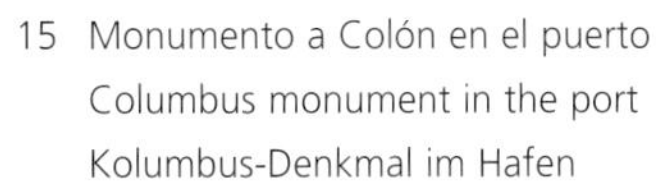

15 Monumento a Colón en el puerto
Columbus monument in the port
Kolumbus-Denkmal im Hafen

↑

16 Rambla de Mar
Rambla de Mar
Rambla de Mar

↑

17 "Golondrina" surcando el puerto
"Golondrina" pleasure-boat leaving the port
„Golondrina" im Hafen

→

18 Teleférico
Cable car
Seilbahn

II

19 Panorámica de la Rambla de Santa Mònica
View of the Rambla de Santa Mònica
Ausblick auf die Rambla de Santa Mònica

20 El corazón de la ciudad medieval
The heart of the medieval city
Das Herz der mittelalterlichen Stadt

↑

21 Claustro de la Catedral
Cathedral Cloister
Kreuzgang der Kathedrale

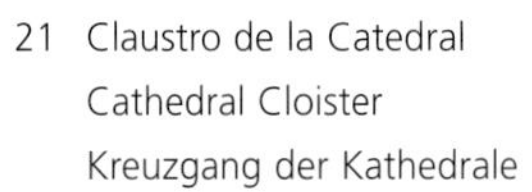

22 Detalle barroco del Palau Dalmases
Baroque detail of the Palau Dalmases
Barockes Detail des Palau Dalmases

↑

23 Plaça del Pi
Plaça del Pi
Plaça del Pi

→

24 Tienda de antigüedades
Antique shop
Antiquitätengeschäft

→→

25 Plaça Reial
Plaça Reial
Plaça Reial

26 La ciudad medieval
The medieval city
Die mittelalterliche Stadt

↑

27 "Castellers" en la Plaça de Sant Jaume
"Castellers" in the Plaça de Sant Jaume
Die „Castellers", Plaça de Sant Jaume

28 Rosetón de la iglesia del Pi
Rose window of the Església del Pi
Rosettenfenster der Església del Pi

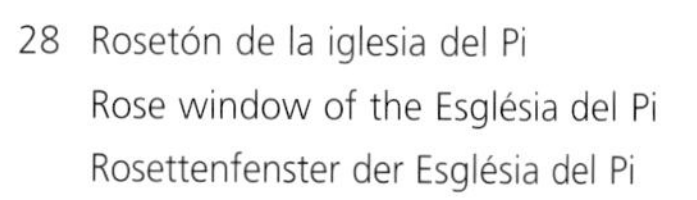

29 Detalle de la fachada de la Catedral
Detail of Cathedral façade
Fassade der Kathedrale

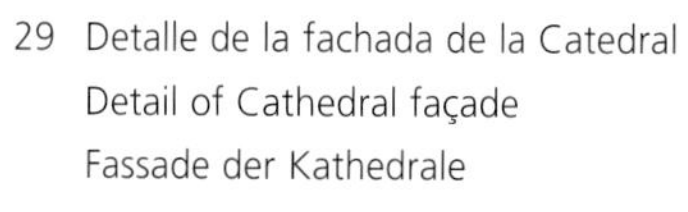

30 La Boqueria
The Boqueria market
La Boqueria

842
843
RAFELS S.A
774

↑

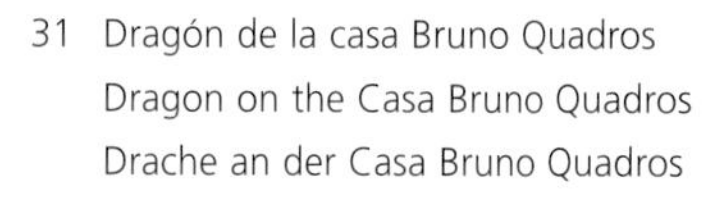

31 Dragón de la casa Bruno Quadros
Dragon on the Casa Bruno Quadros
Drache an der Casa Bruno Quadros

32 Museu d'Història de la Ciutat
The City History Museum
Museu d'Història de la Ciutat

33 Puente gótico de la calle del Bisbe
Gothic bridge in Carrer del Bisbe
Gotischer Übergang, Carrer del Bisbe

34 Baile de gigantes
Dance of the Giants
Tanz der Giganten

HOTEL

35 Buzón de la casa de l'Ardiaca
Letterbox in the Casa de l'Ardiaca
Briefkasten an der Casa de l'Ardiaca

36 Patio del Palau Dalmases
Courtyard of the Palau Dalmases
Innenhof des Palau Dalmases

↑

37 Interior de Santa Maria del Mar
Interior of Santa Maria del Mar
Interieur der Santa Maria del Mar

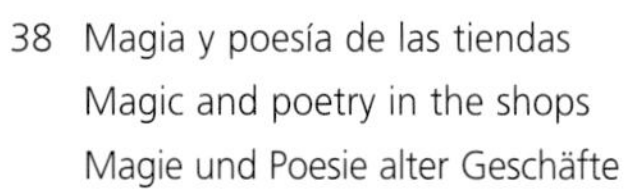

→

38 Magia y poesía de las tiendas
Magic and poetry in the shops
Magie und Poesie alter Geschäfte

EL REY DE LA MAGIA
11
CASA FUNDADA EN 1881
11
MAGIA

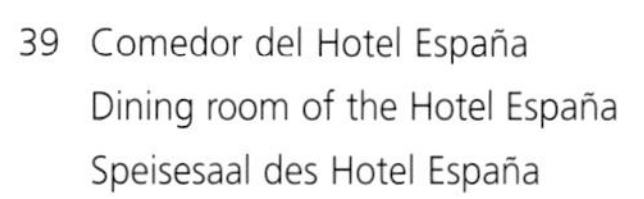

39 Comedor del Hotel España
Dining room of the Hotel España
Speisesaal des Hotel España

40 Gran Teatre del Liceu
Gran Teatre del Liceu
Gran Teatre del Liceu

GENERALI assurances
PANS
487 06 01

←

41 Deportes urbanos
Sport in the city
Sport in der Stadt

↑

42 Playas del litoral
Beaches
Strände

43 Plaça Rovira i Trias
Plaça Rovira i Trias
Plaça Rovira i Trias

44 Instantáneas ciudadanas
City snapshots
Szenen des Stadtlebens

ESCRIBA
PERLAS
MOET
Poble Espanyol
B-6433-GL

↑

45 Frisos esgrafiados de Picasso
Graffito friezes by Picasso
Sgraffito-Malereien Picassos

→

46 *Cap de Barcelona*
Cap de Barcelona
Cap de Barcelona

47 "Pa amb tomàquet"
"Pa amb tomàquet"
„Pa amb tomàquet"

↑

48 Galera Real del Museu Marítim
Royal Galley of the Museu Marítim
„Galera Reial" des Museu Marítim

49 Centre de Cultura Contemporània
The Contemporany Cultura Center
Centre de Cultura Contemporània

50 Dona i Ocell, de Joan Miró
Woman and bird, by Joan Miró
Frau und Vogel, von Joan Miró

51 Columnata del Palau de la Música
Colonnade in the Palau de la Música
Säulengang im Palau de la Música

↑

52 Palau de la Música Catalana
Palau de la Música Catalana
Palau de la Música Catalana

53 Rincón del Eixample
Corner of the Eixample
Ein Winkel der Eixample

54 Escudo del mercado de La Boqueria
Coat of Arms of La Boqueria market
Wappen der Markthalle La Boqueria

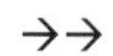

55 Vidriera de la casa Lleó Morera
Stained-glass of the Casa Lleó Morera
Mosaikfenster der Casa Lleó Morera

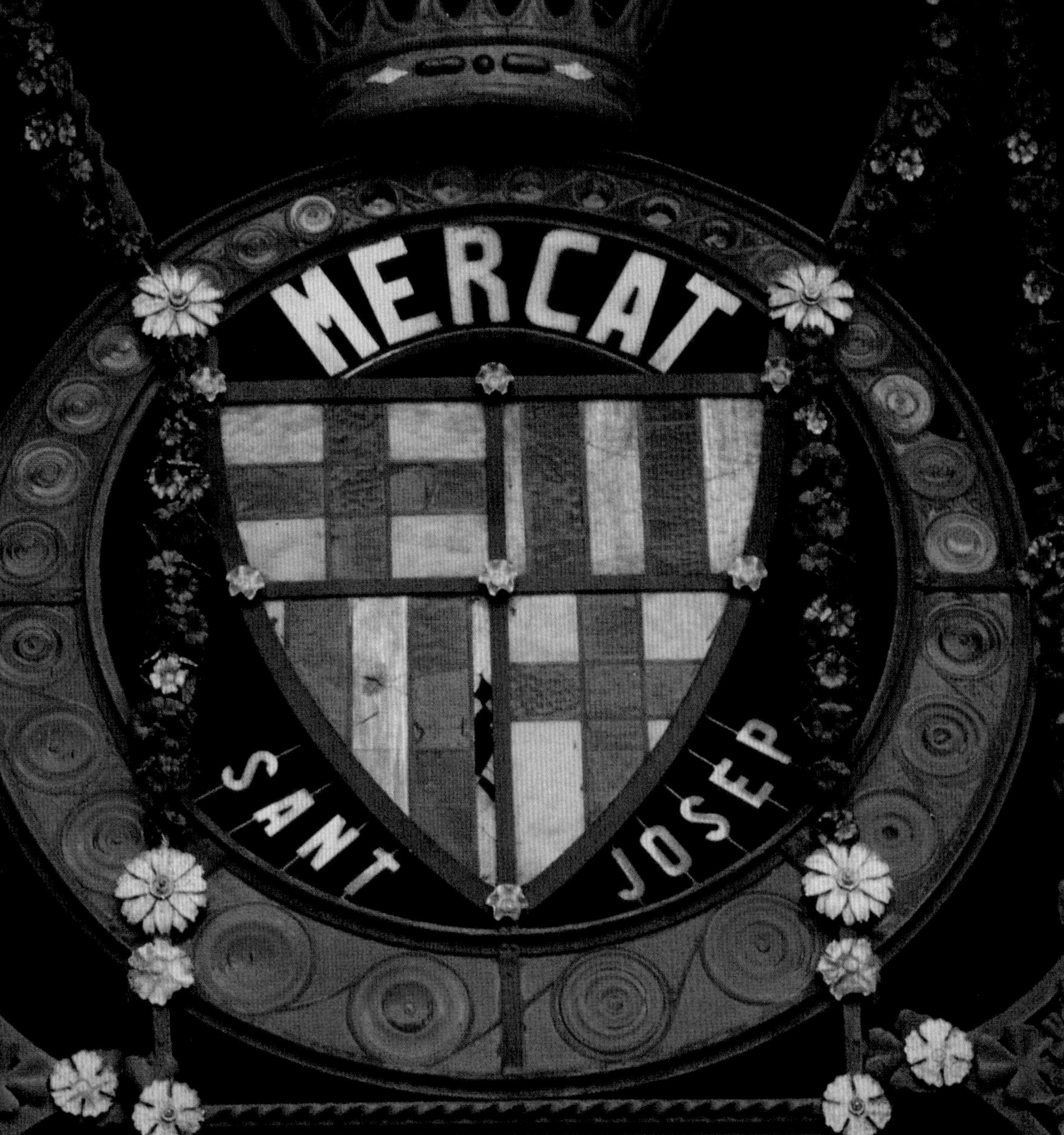
MERCAT
SANT JOSEP
LA BOQUERIA

←

56 "La Pedrera", de Gaudí
"La Pedrera", by Gaudí
„La Pedrera", von Gaudí

↑

57 Balcón-tribuna de la casa Milà
Balcony-gallery of the Casa Milà
Emporenbalkon der Casa Milà

58 Terraza escalonada de la casa Milà
Terraced rooftop of the Casa Milà
Dachterrasse, Casa Milà

↑

59 Casa Batlló
Casa Batlló
Casa Batlló

←

60 Chimeneas de la casa Batlló
Chimneys on the Casa Batlló
Schornsteine der Casa Batlló

↑

61 Interior de la casa Batlló
Interior of the Casa Batlló
Interieur der Casa Batlló

62 Casa Amatller
Casa Amatller
Casa Amatller

63 Detalles modernistas
Modernist details
Jugendstil-Details

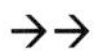

64 Arco de Triunfo
Triumphal Arch
Der Triumphbogen

↑

65 Panorámica aérea de la Sagrada Familia
Aerial view of the Sagrada Família
Luftaufnahme der Sagrada Família

→

66 Detalle de la fachada del Nacimiento
Detail of the Nativity façade
Nahaufnahme der Geburtsfassade

↑

67 Puente entre dos torres
Bridge between two spires
Brücke zwischen zwei Seitentürmen

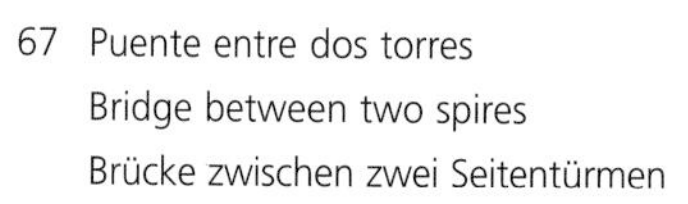

68 Detalles de la Sagrada Familia
Details of the Sagrada Família
Details der Sagrada Família

69 Interior de la Sagrada Familia
Interior of the Sagrada Família
Innenraum der Sagrada Família

70 Fachada de la Pasión
Façade of the Passion
Die Passionsfassade

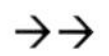

71 Dragón de la escalinata del Park Güell
Dragon on the stairway of Park Güell
Die Drachenskulptur im Park Güell

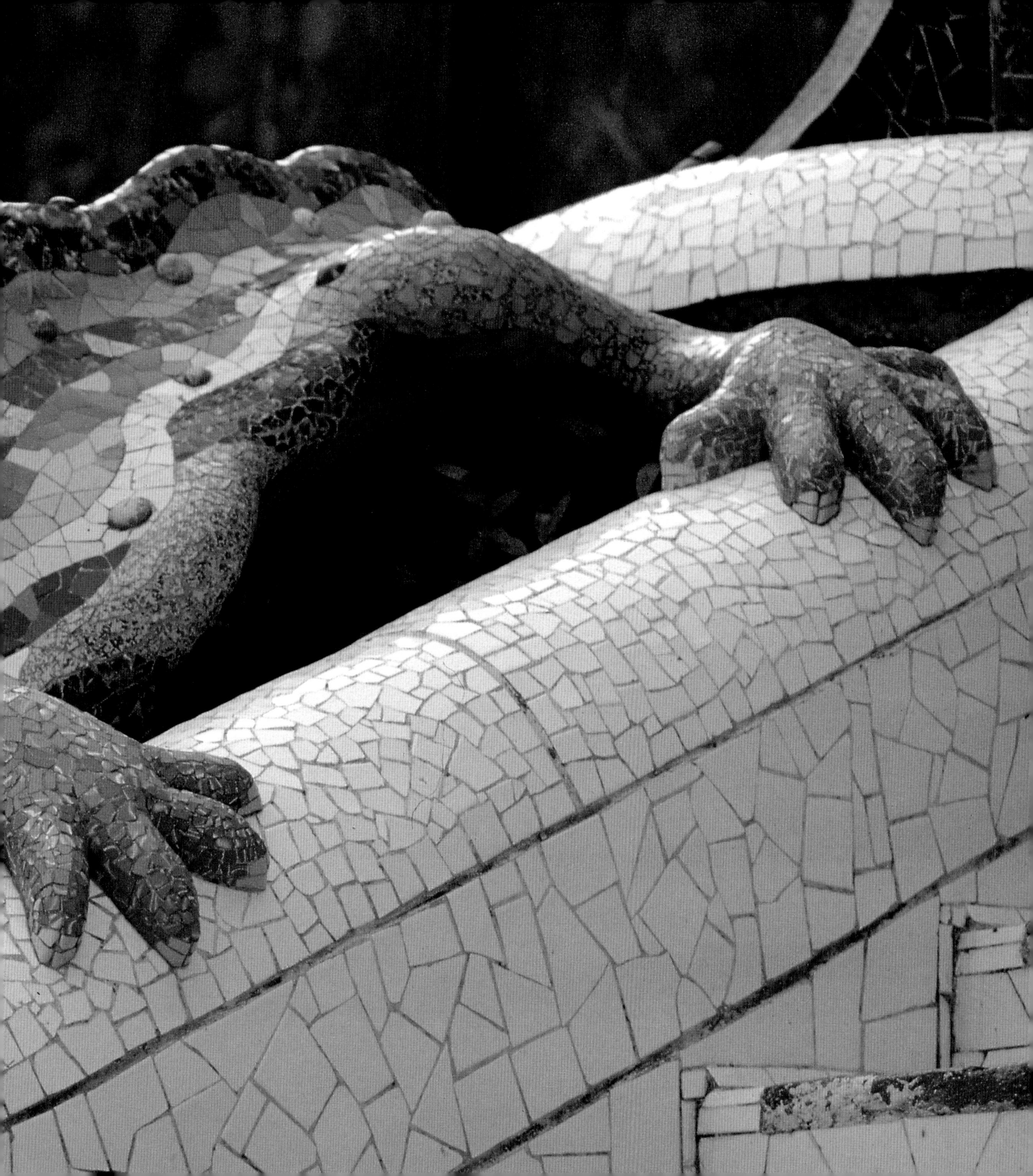

←

72 Un parque protegido por la UNESCO
A park protected by UNESCO
Ein von der UNESCO geschützter Park

↑

73 Banco de la plaza del Park Güell
Serpentine bench in Park Güell
Bank des Platzes im Park Güell

74 Galería porticada del Park Güell
Porched arcade in Park Güell
Säulengang im Park Güell

↑

75 Pabellón del Park Güell
Pavilion in Park Güell
Pavillon im Park Güell

←

76 Jardines del Park Güell
Gardens in Park Güell
Gartenanlagen im Park Güell

↑

77 Columnata dórica. Park Güell
Doric colonnade in Park Güell
Dorische Säulengruppe im Park Güell

78 Casa Vicens
Casa Vicens
Casa Vicens

79 Museu de Zoologia desde el invernáculo
The Museum of Zoology from the greenhouse
Museu de Zoologia, Gewächshaus

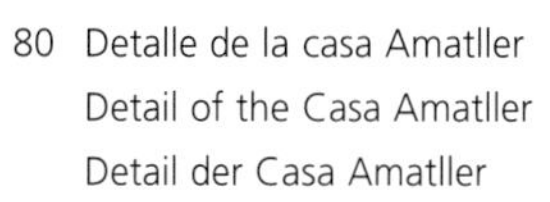

80 Detalle de la casa Amatller
Detail of the Casa Amatller
Detail der Casa Amatller

81 Interior del Palau Macaia
Interior of the Palau Macaia
Interieur des Palau Macaia

82 Escalera de la casa Manuel Felip
Stairway in the Casa Manuel Felip
Treppe in der Casa Manuel Felip

83 La puerta del Dragón. Pavellons Güell
The Dragon Gate at the Güell Pavillions
Drachentor, Pavellons Güell

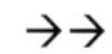

84 Entrada a los Pavellons Güell
Entrance to the Güell Pavillions
Eingang zu den Gut Pavellons Güell

85 Fachada posterior de la casa Comalat
Rear facade of the Casa Comalat
Rückseite der Casa Comalat

86 Interior de Bellesguard
Interior of Bellesguard
Interieur von Bellesguard

↑

87 Reja del Palau Güell
Grille of the Palau Güell
Gitter des Palau Güell

→

88 Terraza del Palau Güell
Terrace of the Palau Güell
Terrasse des Palau Güell

89 Fundació Joan Miró. Montjuïc
The Joan Miró Foundation. Montjuïc
Fundació Joan Miró. Montjuïc

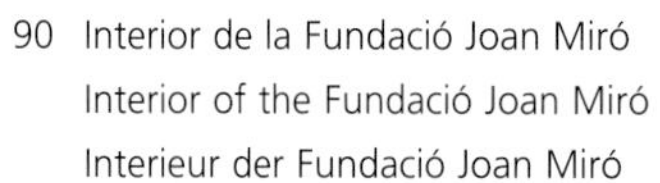

90 Interior de la Fundació Joan Miró
Interior of the Fundació Joan Miró
Interieur der Fundació Joan Miró

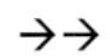

91 Auditori Municipal
The Municipal Auditorium
Auditori Municipal

PAiSTe
MUSSER

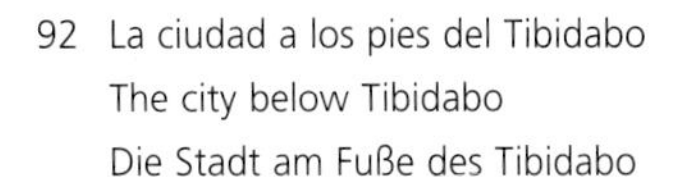

92 La ciudad a los pies del Tibidabo
The city below Tibidabo
Die Stadt am Fuße des Tibidabo

93 Torre de telecomunicaciones
Telecommunication tower
Funkturm

←

94 Bares y locales nocturnos
Bars and nightspots
Bars und Nachtlokale

↑

95 Casa Arnús. "El Pinar"
Casa Arnús. "El Pinar"
Casa Arnús. „El Pinar"

96 Anillo olímpico de Montjuïc
The Olympic Area of Montjuïc
Der Olympiakomplex, Montjuïc

97 Aurigas de Pablo Gargallo
Charioteers by Pablo Gargallo
Wagenlenker von Pablo Gargallo

↑

98 Teatre Nacional de Catalunya
The National Theatre of Catalonia
Teatre Nacional de Catalunya

→

99 Escultura de Georg Kolbe
Sculpture by Georg Kolbe
Skulptur von Georg Kolbe

↑

100 Mamut del Parc de la Ciutadella
Mammoth in Parc de la Ciutadella
Mammut im Parc de la Ciutadella

→

101 Parc del Laberint
Parc del Laberint
Parc del Laberint

↑

102 Puente de Bac de Roda
Bac de Roda Bridge
Die Brücke Bac de Roda

→

103 Parc de l'Espanya Industrial
Parc de l'Espanya Industrial
Parc de l'Espanya Industrial

104 Interior del Aquàrium
Interior of the Aquarium
Im Aquàrium

105 Aquàrium
Aquarium
Aquàrium

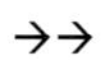

106 Palau Sant Jordi
Palau Sant Jordi
Palau Sant Jordi

l'aquàrium
l'aquàrium
CAIXA 1

←

107 Copito de Nieve, barcelonés ilustre
Floquet de Neu, a citizen of Barcelona
Der berühmte Floquet de Neu

↑

108 Barrio de la Vila Olímpica
The Vila Olímpica
Viertel der Vila Olímpica

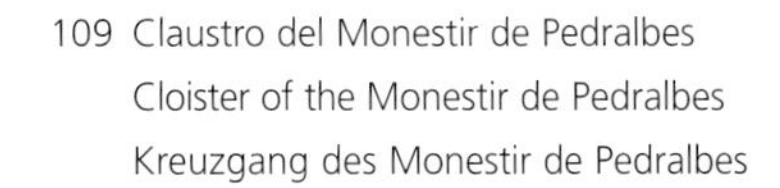

109 Claustro del Monestir de Pedralbes
Cloister of the Monestir de Pedralbes
Kreuzgang des Monestir de Pedralbes

110 *Elogio del agua* de Chillida
In praise of water by Chillida
Lobpreisung des Wassers von Chillida

111 Estadio del Futbol Club Barcelona
Barcelona Football Club Stadium
Stadium des Futbol Club Barcelona

112 Fuego y Diablos
Fire and Devils
Feuer und Teufel

↑

113 Mosaico romano
Roman mosaic
Römisches Mosaik

→

114 Pantocrátor románico
Romanesque Christ Pantocrator
Römischer Pantokrator

115 Fundació Antoni Tapies
The Antoni Tapies Foundation
Fundació Antoni Tapies

116 Patio central del Museu Picasso
Central courtyard of the Picasso Museum
Zentraler Innenhof des Museu Picasso

	Español	English	Deutsch
	1 Cuadrícula del Eixample La cuadrícula planificada por Ildefons Cerdà preveía las futuras necesidades que podría plantear el crecimiento de Barcelona. Intereses egoístas impidieron que el más atrevido proyecto urbanístico de la ciudad moderna se realizara en su totalidad según la concepción original.	The quadrangles of the Eixample The squared urban planning by Ildefons Cerdà foresaw the future needs of the growing city. A conflict of interests prevented this most ambitious project for a modern city from being completed in accordance with the original plans.	Quadratisches Straßennetz des Eixample Bei dem Straßengeflecht im Entwurf des Architekten Ildefons Cerdà für die Stadterweiterung waren bereits die künftigen Bedürfnisse der wachsenden Stadt berücksichtigt. Egoistische Interessen verhinderten jedoch die vollständige Umsetzung eines der kühnsten Projekte moderner Stadtplanung.
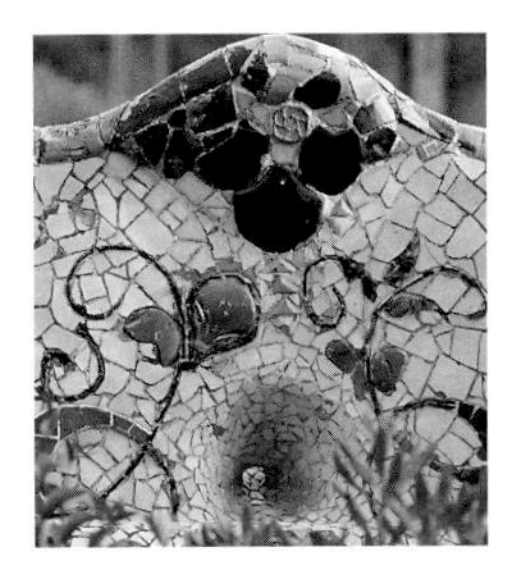	2 Detalle del banco del Park Güell El "trencadís" del banco, de múltiples colores e insólitas formas, es una muestra de las fructíferas colaboraciones entre Gaudí y Josep Mª Jujol, aunque no deben descartarse las aportaciones espontáneas de los artesanos que lo construyeron.	Detail of the bench in Park Güell The "trencadís" of the bench, in multicoloured and unusual shapes, is an example of the fruitful collaboration between Gaudí and Josep Mª Jujol, although contributions from the craftsmen who actually built it should not be ruled out.	Nahaufnahme der Bank im Park Güell Das „Trencadís" der Bank in vielen Farben und einzigartigen Formen ist ein Beispiel für die fruchtbare Zusammen-arbeit zwischen Gaudí und Josep M. Jujol, auch wenn man die spontanen Beiträge der Kunsthandwerker, die sie gebaut haben, nicht vergessen sollte.
	3 El Port Olímpic desde la escollera El Port Olímpic figura ahora como eje central del reencuentro de la ciudad con el mar, un nuevo espacio de gran aceptación para toda clase de actividades de ocio y recreo.	The Port Olímpic from the breakwater The Port Olímpic now features as the central meeting point between the city and the sea, a new space that is very popular for all kinds of leisure and recreational activities.	Blick von der Mole auf den Port Olímpic Der Port Olímpic ist heute die zentrale Achse, an der die Stadt wieder auf das Meer trifft. Der Hafen ist eine neue, sehr beliebte Zone mit einem reichen Freizeit- und Vergnügungsangebot.
	4 Pasarela del Port Vell Concebida como una nueva rambla del mar, la pasarela móvil enlaza el Moll de la Fusta con el Moll d'Espanya, y consigue integrar esta nueva área de ocio al resto de la ciudad.	Port Vell footbridge Designed as a new marine Rambla, the moving footbridge connects Moll de la Fusta with Moll d'Espanya, integrating this leisure area into the rest of the city.	Fußgängerbrücke im Port Vell Die bewegliche Fußgängerbrücke, die wie eine neue Rambla im Meer entworfen wurde, verbindet das Moll de la Fusta mit dem Moll d'Espanya, und schafft so eine Integration zwischen dieser neuen Freizeitzone und dem Rest der Stadt.
	5 Rambla de les Flors Desde siempre la Rambla ha sido la expresión del ritmo ciudadano, un espectáculo inagotable de gente y colorido en el largo trayecto hasta el mar.	Rambla de les Flors La Rambla has always represented the city's heartbeat, an untiring spectacle of people and colour that winds its way down to the sea.	Rambla de les Flors La Rambla war immer schon Ausdruck des Rhythmus der Stadt, ein unaufhörliches, buntes Schauspiel, das sich bis zum Meer hin fortsetzt.

6 Nocturno en la terraza de "La Pedrera"

La noche aumenta la fuerza expresiva de la terraza de La Pedrera y reviste cada uno de sus elementos de un aire mágico y fantasmagórico.

Nightfall on the terrace of "La Pedrera"

The evening view of the terrace of La Pedrera increases its expressive strength and covers each element with a magical and phantasmagorical air.

Abenddämmerung auf der Terrasse der „Pedrera"

Nachts wird die Terrasse der Pedrera noch ausdrucksvoller. Alle Elemente wirken fantastisch und gespenstisch.

7 Porta de la Pau

En la plaza de la Porta de la Pau coinciden el arranque de la Rambla junto al monumento a Colón y las importantísimas atarazanas medievales, sede del Museu Marítim.

Porta de la Pau

The square of the Porta de la Pau coincides with the beginning of La Rambla alongside the Columbus monument and the extremely important medieval arsenal, today the Museu Marítim.

Porta de la Pau

Auf dem Platz Porta de la Pau, an dem La Rambla beginnt, befinden sich das Denkmal an Kolumbus und die mittelalterlichen Werften, welche heute Sitz des Museu Marítim sind.

8 Interior del Estadio Olímpico

Los jinetes del escultor Pablo Gargallo presiden las numerosas actividades deportivas que se celebran a lo largo de todo el año en el Estadio Olímpico

Interior of the Olympic Stadium

The horsemen by the sculptor Pablo Gargallo overlook the many sporting events held throughout the year in the Olympic Stadium.

Olympiastadium von innen

Die Reiterstatuen des Bildhauers Pablo Gargallo beherrschen die zahlreichen Sportveranstaltungen, die das ganze Jahr über im Olympiastadium stattfinden.

9 Miró en el Pla de l'Os

El mosaico de Joan Miró, un homenaje del artista a los paseantes, señala el punto intermedio del sinuoso trayecto de la Rambla.

Miró in the Pla de l'Os

The mosaic by Joan Miró marks the centre of the sinuous route taken by La Rambla, a tribute by the artist to passers-by.

Miró am Pla de l'Os

Das Mosaik von Joan Miró befindet sich in der Mitte des letzten, abfallenden Abschnitts die Rambla, eine Hommage des Künstlers an die Vorbeigehenden.

10 Palau de la Música Catalana

Templo del modernismo catalán, el Palau de la Música puede considerarse el máximo exponente de esta corriente estética. Su sala de conciertos y escenario se concibieron como un espacio único en el que destacan los grupos escultóricos que simbolizan la música popular y la música clásica.

Palau de la Música Catalana

The temple of Modernisme, the Palau is considered by many to be the unrivalled example of the aesthetics of that time. The concert hall and stage were designed as one spacious element in which the groups of sculptures, representing both classical and traditional music, are of particular interest.

Palau de la Música Catalana

Der oft als Tempel des katalanischen Jugendstils bezeichnete Palau de la Música ist zweifellos das wichtigste Beispiel dieser Kunst– und Architekturströmung. Die Skulpturengruppen des in sich abgeschlossenen Konzert– und Theatersaals symbolisieren die klassische und die volkstümliche Musik.

11 "Casa de les Punxes"

La "casa de les Punxes", situada en la Diagonal, entre las calles de Bruc y Llúria, fue resuelta por Puig i Cadafalch en clave neogótica. Tiene la peculiaridad de abarcar una manzana completa del Eixample, lo que le da una cohesión extraordinaria.

"Casa de les Punxes"

The "Casa de les Punxes", situated on the Diagonal between Bruc and Llúria Streets, was built on neo-gothic lines by the architect Puig i Cadafalch. It is unique in that it occupies an entire block of Eixample, providing it with an extraordinary cohesion.

„Casa de les Punxes"

Das auf der Avinguda Diagonal zwischen Carrer Bruc und Carrer Llúria gelegene Haus „Casa de les Punxes" wurde von Puig i Cadafalch im neugotischen Stil erbaut. Das Gebäude nimmt einen ganzen Block des Eixample ein, wodurch es außergewöhnlich geschlossen wirkt.

12 Vista aérea del barrio de la Ribera

Históricamente, este barrio de origen medieval fue el más activo y emprendedor de Barcelona. Conserva su antiguo trazado de calles estrechas y apelmazadas en torno a la protectora iglesia de Santa Maria del Mar.

Aerial view of La Ribera district

Historically, this district of medieval origin was the most active and go-ahead of Barcelona. It still maintains its old network of narrow and tightly-knit streets that surround the protective church of Santa Maria del Mar.

Luftaufnahme vom Viertel La Ribera

Dieses im Mittelalter entstandene Viertel war einst das unternehmerische Zentrum Barcelonas. Die alten, engen Gassen rund um die Kirche Santa Maria del Mar haben sich bis heute erhalten.

13 Museu d'Art Contemporani de Barcelona

La sede del popular MACBA, obra del arquitecto norteamericano Richard Meier, destaca por la peculiar característica de su arquitectura blanca y por la luminosidad y transparencia tan adecuadas a un espacio museístico.

The Museum of Contemporany Art of Barcelona

The headquarters for the popular MACBA, by the North American architect Richard Meier, stands out for its singular white architecture and for the luminosity and transparency so befitting a museum space.

Museu d'Art Contemporani de Barcelona

Das Gebäude des berühmten Museums MACBA, Werk des nordamerikanischen Architekten Richard Meier, fällt durch seine weiße Architektur und durch die Helligkeit und Transparenz auf, die es zu einem ausgezeichneten Sitz für ein Museum machen.

14 Visión nocturna del Port Vell

Una de las zonas más vivas de la ciudad se ha visto ampliada con la incorporación de una parte del Port Vell. Un lugar idóneo para el paseo y la contemplación.

Night view of Port Vell

One of the liveliest areas of the city has been enlarged by the inclusion of part of Port Vell. An ideal spot for strolling and contemplation.

Nächtlicher Blick auf den Port Vell

Eine der lebendigsten Zonen der Stadt wurde durch die Integration eines Teils des Port Vell erweitert. Ein wundervoller Ort für einen besinnlichen Spaziergang.

15 Monumento a Colón en el puerto

Barcelona honra la memoria de Cristóbal Colón con este monumento erigido en 1886, obra del arquitecto Gaietà Buigas, que preside la entrada por mar a la ciudad.

Columbus monument in the port

Barcelona honours the memory of Christopher Columbus with this monument raised in1886, work of the architect Gaietà Buigas, which overlooks the entrance to the city by sea.

Kolumbus-Denkmal im Hafen

Mit diesem Denkmal aus dem Jahre 1886, ein Werk des Architekten Gaietà Buigas, das die Einfahrt in die Stadt vom Meer her überschaut, erinnert Barcelona an Kolumbus.

16 Rambla de Mar

La transformación espectacular del Port Vell ha permitido convertir el puerto en una zona comercial y de ocio ciudadano como el Maremàgnum, llena de cines, tiendas y restaurantes.

Rambla de Mar

The spectacular transformation of Port Vell has enabled the port to be turned into a commercial and leisure area with the Maremàgnum, full of cinemas, shops and restaurants.

Rambla de Mar

Die Aufsehen erregende Umformung des Port Vell machte aus dem Hafen das Einkaufs- und Freizeitzentrum Maremàgnum, wo der Besucher Kinos, Geschäfte und Restaurants findet.

17 "Golondrina" surcando el puerto

Desde las "golondrinas" que trasladan a los pasajeros hasta la escollera se pueden observar con detalle las actividades portuarias.

"Golondrina" pleasure-boat leaving the port

From the "golondrinas" or pleasure-boats that take passengers to the breakwater, the port activities can be seen close-up.

„Golondrina" im Hafen

„Golondrinas" heißen die beliebten Ausflugsboote, die ihren Fahrgästen während der Fahrt zum großen Wellenbrecher die Möglichkeit bieten, die Hafenanlagen zu besichtigen.

18 Teleférico

Otra forma insólita de paseo que permite una perspectiva espléndida sobre la ciudad es el Teleférico, que une la Torre de Sant Sebastià, en el extremo del puerto, con la montaña de Montjuïc.

Cable Car

Another unusual mode of transport that provides a splendid view over the city is the cable car that links the Torre de Sant Sebastià at the end of the port with the Montjuic mountain.

Seilbahn

Eine originelle Spazierfahrt mit einem ausgezeichneten Blick über die Stadt bietet die Seilbahn, welche den Torre de Sant Sebastià am Ende des Hafens mit dem Berg Montjuïc verbindet.

19 Panorámica de la Rambla de Santa Mònica

La parte baja de la Rambla ha experimentado cambios importantes en estos últimos años con el establecimiento de una parte de las dependencias de la Universitat Pompeu Fabra y el Centre d'Art Santa Mónica.

View of the Rambla de Santa Mònica

The lower part of La Rambla has undergone important changes in recent years with the establishment of part of the Universitat Pompeu Fabra and the Centre d'Art Santa Mònica.

Ausblick auf die Rambla de Santa Mònica

Der untere Teil La Rambla hat sich in den letzten Jahren stark verändert. Dort wurden ein Teil der Anlagen der Universität Pompeu Fabra und das Kunstzentrum Centre d'Art Santa Mònica untergebracht.

20 El corazón de la ciudad medieval

El Mirador del Rei Martí, perteneciente al antiguo Palau Reial Major, señala el centro del Barri Gòtic; junto a él, en primer plano, la parte superior del Palau del Lloctinent, del siglo XVI.

The heart of the medieval city

The Mirador del Rei Martí, belonging to the ancient Palau Reial Major, marks the centre of the Barri Gòtic. Alongside it, in the foreground, the upper part of the 16th century Palau del Lloctinent.

Das Herz der mittelalterlichen Stadt

Vom Aussichtspunkt Rei Martí, Teil des alten Palau Reial Major (Königspalast), blickt man mitten ins Barri Gòtic. Im Vordergrund der obere Teil des Palastes Palau del Lloctinent aus dem XVI. Jahrhundert.

21 Claustro de la Catedral

Cuatro galerías con bóveda de crucería y verjas de hierro forjado delimitan el jardín interior con palmeras y magnolios del claustro de la catedral. El rumor del agua de la fuente gótica, la luz tamizada y la presencia de las ocas lo convierten en uno de los lugares más hermosos de la ciudad.

Cathedral Cloister

Four cross-vaulted galleries with wrought iron railings encircle the inner garden. Palm trees and magnolias, the babbling water from the Gothic fountain, the filtered light and the presence of the geese make this one of the most beautiful spots of the city.

Kreuzgang der Kathedrale

Vier Galerien mit Kreuzgewölben und schmiedeeiserne Gitter umgeben den Palmen– und Magnoliengarten des Kreuzgangs im Innenhof der Kathedrale. Das Plätschern des gotischen Brunnens, das Spiel von Licht und Schatten und die hier lebenden Gänse machen aus ihm einen der schönsten Orte der Stadt.

22 Detalle barroco del Palau Dalmases

La escalera de honor del patio interior del Palau Dalmases es una obra maestra de la escultura barroca catalana. Las columnas salomónicas están adornadas con "putti", como el que aquí vemos, y parras enroscadas.

Baroque detail of the Palau Dalmases

The main stairway of the inner courtyard of the Palau Dalmases is a masterpiece of Catalan Baroque sculpture. The Solomonic columns are adorned with "putti", as we see here, and coiled vines.

Barockes Detail des Palau Dalmases

Die Haupttreppe im Innenhof des Palau Dalmases stellt ein Meisterwerk barocker katalanischer Bildhauerei dar. Die gewundenen Säulen sind, wie die hier abgebildete, mit „Putti" verziert, und mit sich windenden Weinreben.

23 Plaça del Pi

La Plaça del Pi, una de las más queridas por los barceloneses, ve aumentado su encanto por la ausencia de tráfico motorizado. Alternando horas de calma y bullicio, es punto de confluencia obligado para los visitantes del casco antiguo.

Plaça del Pi

The Plaça del Pi, one of the most loved squares by the people of Barcelona, is even more pleasant when you consider there is no traffic here. Sometimes quiet, sometimes a busy hive of activity, it is an absolute must for visitors to the Gothic Quarter.

Plaça del Pi

Die Plaça del Pi ist sehr beliebt bei den Einwohnern der Stadt. Was diesen Ort noch angenehmer macht, ist die Tatsache, dass es kaum Verkehr gibt. Ruhe und Betriebsamkeit wechseln sich dort ab, ein Abstecher zu diesem Platz während des Besuches der Altstadt ist fast obligatorisch.

24 Tienda de antigüedades

En el Barri Gòtic abundan las tiendas de antigüedades que con su presencia contribuyen a la ambientación y al encanto de sus calles y plazas.

Antique shop

The presence of many antique shops in the Barri Gòtic contributes to the charm and atmosphere of the streets and squares.

Antiquitätengeschäft

Im Barri Gòtic, dem historischen Gotischen Viertel, finden sich viele Antiquitätengeschäfte, die das typische Flair und den eigentümlichen Zauber seiner Strassen und Plätze noch erhöhen.

25 Plaça Reial

Presenta un aspecto uniforme gracias a que los edificios porticados que la delimitan respetan el diseño original de plaza cerrada, inspirado en el urbanismo francés. La fuente, las dos farolas diseñadas por Gaudí y las palmeras alegran una de las plazas con más carácter de Barcelona.

Plaça Reial

The Plaça Reial offers this uniform aspect as all the porticoed buildings around it respect the original French design of a closed square.
The fountain, the street lamps designed by Gaudí and the palm trees enhance what is one of the most lively squares in the city.

Plaça Reial

Die Gebäude rund um die Plaça Reial folgen mit ihren Arkaden ausnahmslos dem ursprünglichen Konzept des geschlossenen Platzes nach französischem Muster. Der Brunnen, die von Gaudí entworfenen Laternen und die Palmen beleben diesen Platz, der wohl einer der charakteristischsten der Stadt ist.

26 La ciudad medieval

Los perfiles de la Catedral, del Palau Reial Major y la capilla de Santa Àgueda destacan su presencia de siglos en la oscuridad de la noche. El centro histórico de Barcelona se alza sobre los restos de la ciudad romana en este rincón de las antiguas murallas.

The medieval city

The profiles of the Cathedral, the Palau Reial Major and the chapel of Santa Àgueda mark their centuries-old presence in the darkness of the night. Barcelona's historic centre is raised over the Roman city in this corner of the ancient walled settlement.

Die mittelalterliche Stadt

Die Silhouetten der Kathedrale, des Palau Reial Major und der Kapelle Santa Àgueda ragen in die Dunkelheit der Nacht, wie sie es schon seit Jahrhunderten tun. Das historische Zentrum Barcelonas erhebt sich über den Ruinen der römischen Stadt zwischen den alten Stadtmauern.

27 "Castellers" en la Plaça de Sant Jaume

Durante la celebración de fiestas populares como las de la Mercè, patrona de la ciudad, se realizan múltiples actos y festejos en los que las viejas tradiciones tienen un papel relevante. Aquí vemos cómo se corona un "castell" frente al Ayuntamiento.

"Castellers" in the Plaça de Sant Jaume

Old traditions play an important role during many popular festivals such as la Mercè, the patron saint of the city. Here we see how a "castell", or human tower, is successfully accomplished in front of the Town Hall.

Die „Castellers", Plaça de Sant Jaume

Während der Volksfeste wie dem Fest zu Ehren von Mercè, der Schutzheiligen Barcelonas, finden zahlreiche Festakte statt, in deren Mittelpunkt althergebrachte Traditionen stehen. Hier sieht man, wie vor dem Rathaus ein „castell", ein menschlicher Turm, vollendet wird.

28 Rosetón de la iglesia del Pi

El rosetón de tracería foliada de la iglesia de Santa Maria dels Reis, o del Pi, del siglo XIV, tiene unas dimensiones inusuales dentro de la arquitectura gótica religiosa; se dice que es el más grande del mundo.

Rose window of the Església del Pi

The rose window of the 14th century Church of Santa Maria dels Reis (or del Pi), with its foliate design, has unusual dimensions for a work of religious Gothic architecture. It is said to be the largest in the world.

Rosettenfenster der Kirche del Pi

Das Rosettenfenster der Kirche Santa Maria dels Reis oder del Pi (14. – 15. Jh.) hat eine für die religiöse gotische Architektur ungewöhnliche Größe. Man sagt sogar, es sei das größte seiner Art auf der Welt.

29 Detalle de la fachada de la Catedral

La fachada de la Catedral, proyectada a finales del siglo XIX, no se corresponde históricamente con el resto de la construcción, erigida entre los siglos XIII y XV, si bien sigue fielmente el dibujo gótico que se conserva en el archivo catedralicio, fechado en 1408.

Detail of Cathedral façade

The 19th century façade does not tally with the rest of the Cathedral, built between the 13th and 15th centuries.
It does, however, correspond to the original Gothic plans, dated 1408, that are preserved in the Cathedral archives.

Fassade der Kathedrale

Die Fassade der Kathedrale stammt vom Ende des 19. Jahrhunderts, also nicht aus der eigentlichen Bauzeit der Kathedrale (13. – 15. Jh.) . Allerdings hielt man sich bei der Gestaltung der Fassade getreu an den im Kirchenarchiv erhaltenen, gotischen Originalplan aus dem Jahre 1408.

30 La Boqueria

El dragón chino perteneciente al edificio orientalista de Josep Vilaseca, situado en el Pla de la Boqueria, se hermana con los numerosos dragones que aparecen por toda la geografía urbana barcelonesa.

The Boqueria market

The route along La Rambla deserves an obligatory stop-off to enter into La Boqueria market, which is to penetrate into the kingdom of aromas and colours and of the suggestive forms and textures of the foods on display.

Der Markt La Boqueria

Beim Spaziergang über La Rambla muss auf jeden Fall ein Halt am Mercat de la Boqueria vorgesehen werden. Das ist wie ein Eindringen in das Reich der Düfte und Farben, der verführerischen Formen und Texturen der Speisen.

31 Dragón de la casa Bruno Quadros

El dragón chino perteneciente al edificio orientalista de Josep Vilaseca, situado en el Pla de la Boqueria, se hermana con los numerosos dragones que aparecen por toda la geografía urbana barcelonesa.

Dragon on the Casa Bruno Quadros

The Chinese dragon protruding from Josep Vilaseca's oriental style building in the Pla de la Boqueria is brother to the many dragons that are dispersed all over the city.

Drache an der Casa Bruno Quadros

Der chinesische Drachen des am Pla de la Boqueria auf den Rambles gelegenen, orientalischen Gebäudes des Architekten Josep Vilaseca ist nur einer der vielen Drachen, die man in der ganzen Stadt Barcelona finden kann.

32 Museu d'Història de la Ciutat

El subsuelo del conjunto monumental de la Plaça del Rei conserva los restos arqueológicos de la ciudad romana desde el siglo I. Poco a poco los misterios de la antigua Barcino se han ido desvelando.

The City History Museum

The subsoil of the monuments inhabiting the Plaça del Rei preserve the archaeological remains of the Roman city dating from the 1st century AC. Little by little, the mysteries of the ancient city of Barcino are being unwrapped.

Museu d'Història de la Ciutat

Unter der historischen Plaça del Rei befinden sich die Reste der Römischen Stadt aus dem 1. Jahrhundert n. C. Allmählich werden die Geheimnisse der alten Stadt Barcino aufgedeckt.

33 Puente gótico de la calle del Bisbe

Aunque de construcción moderna, el puente que une el Palau de la Generalitat a las antiguas Cases dels Canonges acentúa la coherencia de esta parte del Barri Gòtic, próxima a la plaza de Sant Jaume.

Gothic bridge in Carrer del Bisbe

Although of more recent construction, the bridge joining the Palau de la Generalitat and the old Cases dels Canonges emphasises the coherence of this part of the Barri Gòtic, close to the Plaça de Sant Jaume.

Gotischer Übergang, carrer Bisbe

Obwohl erst in diesem Jahrhundert erbaut, akzentuiert der überdachte Übergang vom Palau de la Generalitat zu den Cases dels Canonges das harmonische Gefüge dieses Teils des Barri Gótic, in unmittelbarer Nähe des Plaça de Sant Jaume.

34 Baile de gigantes

Todas las celebraciones populares que tienen un marcado carácter tradicional se ven animadas con la participación de los gigantes de la ciudad.

Dance of the Giants

All the popular festivals of a traditional nature are livened up by the participation of the city's giants.

Tanz der Giganten

Die Giganten der Stadt, "Els Gegants", sorgen auf jedem Volksfest traditionellen Charakters für Unterhaltung.

35 Buzón de la Casa de l'Ardiaca

Los orígenes de la Casa de l'Ardiaca se remontan al siglo XII, pero el conjunto actual pertenece a las reformas realizadas en siglo XVI. El buzón de mármol, con los motivos simbólicos del vuelo de pájaros y la tortuga, fue proyectado por Domènech i Montaner a principios del siglo XX.

Letterbox in the Casa de l'Ardiaca

The origins of the Casa de l'Ardiaca are to be found in the 12th century, but what we see today is the result of the 16th century renovation. The marble letterbox, decorated with symbolic motifs of flying birds and the tortoise, was designed by Domènech i Montaner in the early 20th century.

Briefkasten an der Casa de l'Ardiaca

Das Haus Casa de l'Ardiaca hat seinen Ursprung zwar im 12. Jahrhundert, doch seine jetzige Form geht auf einen Umbau im 16. Jahrhundert zurück. Der Marmorbriefkasten mit der Vogelflug– und Schildkrötensymbolik wurde von Domènech i Montaner zu Beginn des 20. Jahrhunderts entworfen.

36 Patio del Palau Dalmases

La reforma en el siglo XVII, de un antiguo palacio del siglo XV determinó el actual Palau Dalmases, cuyo patio interior contiene la espléndida escalera barroca porticada. En la actualidad es sede de Omnium Cultural, entidad promotora de la cultura catalana.

Courtyard of the Palau Dalmases

The renovation of a 15th century palace gave rise to the 17th century Palau Dalmases whose inner courtyard contains the remarkable Baroque stairway with porches.
Today the palace houses the Omnium Cultural, an organisation promoting Catalan culture.

Innenhof des Palau Dalmases

Der Palau Dalmases, in dessen Innenhof sich diese herrliche Barocktreppe befindet, entstand im 17. Jahrhundert durch die Umgestaltung eines älteren Palastes (15. Jh.). Gegenwärtig beherbergt er den Sitz von Omnium Cultural, einer Gesellschaft zur Förderung der katalanischen Kultur.

37 Interior de Santa Maria del Mar

La iglesia basílica de Santa Maria del Mar, del siglo XIV, reúne las mejores características y proporciones del gótico catalán. Este templo se convirtió en el nuevo centro espiritual de un barrio de mercaderes y armadores empeñados en la expansión por el Mediterráneo.

Interior of Santa Maria del Mar

The 14th century basilica of Santa Maria del Mar brings together the finest features and proportions of Catalan Gothic architecture. This church became the new spiritual centre of a district of merchants and shipowners keen to expand their activity across the Mediterranean.

Interieur der Santa Maria del Mar

Die Kirche Santa Maria del Mar (14. Jh.) vereint in sich beispielhaft die typischen Merkmale der katalanischen Gotik. Die Kirche war geistliches Zentrum eines Viertels von Kaufleuten und Reedern, die energisch die Expansion Kataloniens im westlichen Mittelmeer vorantrieben.

38 Magia y poesía de las tiendas

Por toda la ciudad antigua podemos encontrar tiendas cargadas de historia, de encanto y de poesía. Locales que han sido y son artífices de buena parte del carácter de un barrio.

Magic and poetry in the shops

Throughout the old part of the city, one comes across shops that are full of history, charm and poetry. These shops have formed an integral part of the district's character and personality.

Magie und Poesie alter Geschäfte

In der ganzen Altstadt finden sich bezaubernde alte Geschäfte voller Nostalgie und Poesie, die den Charakter dieses Viertels prägten und noch immer prägen.

39 Comedor del Hotel España

Domènech i Montaner decoró este comedor en pleno auge del modernismo. Los motivos marinos acompañan a las delicadas sirenas en las pinturas de la pared; y en el arrimadero, de madera y cerámica, se reproducen los escudos de los antiguos reinos, señoríos y ciudades españolas.

Dining room of the Hotel España

Domènech i Montaner decorated this dining room during the Modernist movement's age of splendour. The marine motifs accompany the delicate nymphs in the wall paintings, and along the wainscot, made from wood and ceramics, different Spanish coats of arms are reproduced.

Speisesaal des Hotel España

Der Architekt Domènech i Montaner gestaltete diesen Saal in der Blütezeit des Modernismus. Meerestiere und zierliche Nixen bilden das Hauptmotiv des Wandgemäldes. Die Holz- und Keramikvertäfelung zeigt die Wappen alter Königreiche, Rittertümer oder spanischer Städte.

40 Gran Teatre del Liceu

La reconstrucción del Gran Teatre del Liceu fue una de las prioridades culturales más acuciantes en estos últimos años. El resultado, de una fidelidad asombrosa, ha permitido reproducir las excepcionales condiciones acústicas y reanudar así la actividad operística, tan representativa de la ciudad.

Gran Teatre del Liceu

The rebuilding of the Liceu was one of the most pressing cultural priorities of recent years. The result, incredibly loyal to its predecessor, means that the fantastic acoustic conditions have been reproduced and opera can once again be staged, an activity so representative of the city.

Gran Teatre del Liceu

Der Wiederaufbau des Theaters Gran Teatre del Liceu war eines der wichtigsten, kulturellen Projekte der letzten Jahre. Durch die originalgetreue Renovierung konnten die optimalen akustischen Bedingungen wieder hergestellt und so die Oper wieder ein Teil des Kulturlebens der Stadt werden.

41 Deportes urbanos

El grado de aceptación popular de toda clase de convocatorias deportivas abiertas no ha hecho más que crecer entre los barceloneses. Los escenarios urbanos acogen una y otra vez a los participantes entusiastas.

Sport in the city

The tremendous popularity of all types of open sporting events has grown and grown amongst the inhabitants of Barcelona. The urban settings play host to the enthusiastic participants time and time again.

Sport in der Stadt

Das Interesse für alle Arten von Sportereignissen wächst in Barcelona ständig. In den städtischen Sportanlagen sind die sportbegeisterten Teilnehmer stets willkommen.

42 Playas

La reordenación del frente marítimo ha permitido ganar una nueva franja costera de playas que se extienden hasta la desembocadura del río Besòs, como las de Icària, Bogatell o las de la Mar Bella.

Beaches

The reorganisation of the seafront has enabled the city to gain a new coastal area of beaches that extend as far as the mouth of the river Besòs, such as those of Icària, Bogatell or Mar Bella.

Strände

Durch die urbanistische Erneuerung der Küstenlinie entstanden neue Strände für die Stadt mit so klangvollen Namen wie Icària, Bogatell und Mar Bella, die sich bis zur Mündung des Flusses Besòs hinziehen.

43 Plaça Rovira i Trias

El barrio de Gràcia perpetúa con este monumento la figura de Antoni Rovira i Trias, arquitecto y urbanista ganador del concurso para el Eixample de Barcelona que luego sería adjudicado a Ildefons Cerdà.

Plaça Rovira i Trias

With this monument, the Gràcia district pays homage to the figure of Antoni Rovira i Trias, architect and urban planner who won the competition to build the Eixample district of Barcelona which was later awarded to Ildefons Cerdà.

Plaça Rovira i Trias

Der Stadtteil Gracià erinnert mit diesem Denkmal an Antoni Rovira i Trias, den Architekten, der den Wettbewerb für die Gestaltung der Stadterweiterung gewonnen hatte, wenngleich deren Ausführung dann Ildefons Cerdà übertragen wurde.

44 Instantáneas ciudadanas

Espacios lúdicos, locales tradicionales, omnipresencia del tráfico motorizado..., entre éstas y otras muchas situaciones transcurre la vida de los barceloneses.

City snapshots

Leisure spaces, traditional spots, the ever present motorised traffic. Among these and many other situations, inhabitants of Barcelona live their daily lives.

Szenen des Stadtlebens

Spielplätze, traditionelle Lokale, allgegenwärtiger Straßenverkehr..., Szenen wie diese bestimmten das Alltagsleben der Bewohner Barcelonas.

45 Frisos esgrafiados de Picasso

Los grandes frisos esgrafiados, diseñados por Pablo Picasso para el Colegio de Arquitectos en la Plaça Nova, presiden la gran explanada frente a la Catedral, en pleno centro histórico de la ciudad.

Graffito friezes by Picasso

The large graffito friezes, designed by Pablo Picasso for the Architect's School in the Plaça Nova, overlook the grand esplanade facing the Cathedral, right in the historic centre of the city.

Sgraffito-Malereien Picassos

Die großen Sgraffito-Malereien Picassos an der Architektenkammer auf der Plaça Nova schmücken den großen Vorplatz der Kathedrale in der historischen Altstadt von Barcelona.

46 *Cap de Barcelona*

El pintor norteamericano Roy Lichtenstein concibió esta escultura, pensada especialmente para Barcelona y situada en uno de los extremos del Moll de la Fusta, dentro de su peculiar estilo vinculado al Pop Art.

Cap de Barcelona

The North American painter Roy Lichtenstein designed this sculpture specially for Barcelona and situated at one of the ends of Moll de la Fusta, within his unique Pop Art style.

Cap de Barcelona

Der nordamerikanische Maler Roy Lichtenstein entwarf diese Skulptur am Ende des Moll de la Fusta speziell für die Stadt Barcelona. Ein typisches Beispiel für seinen von der Pop-Art beeinflussten Stil.

47 "Pa amb tomàquet"

A cualquier hora, solo o acompañado, el pan con tomate es un plato apetitoso. De todos los platos típicos de la cocina catalana, ninguno se le puede comparar en popularidad.

"Pa amb tomàquet"

At all hours, on its own or accompanied, "pa amb tomàquet", bread and tomato, is a delicious dish. No typical Catalan dish can compare with its popularity.

„Pa amb tomàquet"

Ob allein oder als Beilage zu anderen Speisen - von allen typischen Elementen der katalanischen Küche ist das „Brot mit Tomate" sicher das beliebteste.

48 Galera Real del Museu Marítim

El Museu Marítim, situado en las atarazanas del siglo XIV, junto al puerto, es crónica viva del pasado marítimo de la ciudad. La Galera Real de don Juan de Austria, capitán general en la batalla de Lepanto, fue reproducida en los mismos astilleros donde había sido construida en el siglo XVI.

Royal Galley of the Museu Marítim

The Maritime Museum, situated in the 14th century Drassanes, or arsenal, next to the port, is a living chronicle of the city's naval past. The Royal Galley of Juan of Austria, Admiral of the Fleet at the Battle of Lepant, was reproduced in the same dockyards as the 16th century original.

„Galera Real" des Museu Marítim

Das am Hafen gelegene Seefahrtmuseum in „Les Drassanes" (14. Jh.) stellt eine lebendige Chronik der von der Seefahrt bestimmten Vergangenheit der Stadt dar. Die königliche Galeere von Don Juan de Austria, dem Oberbefehlshaber der Schlacht von Lepanto, wurde in der gleichen Werft nachgebaut, in der sie im 16. Jahrhundert konstruiert wurde.

49 Centre de Cultura Contemporània

El Centre de Cultura Contemporània de Barcelona (CCCB), situado en la antigua Casa de la Caritat, obra de los arquitectos Helio Piñón y Marc Viaplana, fue concebido como un centro multidisciplinar, y está entre los que registran mayor actividad cultural.

The Contemporany Culture Centre

The Contemporany Culture Centre of Barcelona (CCCB), situated in the old Casa de la Caritat, was designed by the architects Helio Piñón and Marc Viaplana, and designed as a multidisciplinary centre and among those that play host to a high level of cultural activity.

Centre de Cultura Contemporània

Das Kulturzentrum Centre de Cultura Contemporània de Barcelona (CCCB) in der ehemaligen Casa de la Caritat ist ein Werk der Architekten Helio Piñon und Marc Viaplana. Es handelt sich um ein multidisziplinäres Zentrum, das zahlreiche kulturelle Aktivitäten anbietet.

50 *Dona i Ocell*, de Joan Miró

La escultura *Dona i Ocell* preside el Parc Joan Miró, o del Escorxador, próximo al recinto de Montjuïc. Los motivos temáticos se complementan en esta soberbia escultura con los colores más representativos del autor.

Woman and bird by Joan Miró

The *Dona i Ocell* (woman and bird) sculpture overlooks the Parc Joan Miró, or the Escorxador, nearby the Montjuïc area. The thematic motifs and typical colours used by the artist combine in this superb sculpture.

Frau und Vogel, von Joan Miró

Die Skulptur *Dona i Ocell* (Frau und Vogel) beherrscht den Parc Joan Miró oder Escorxador in der Nähe des Montjuïc. Die Titelmotive dieser prächtigen Skulptur spielen mit den für den Künstler typischen Farben.

51 Columnata del Palau de la Música

La ornamentación característica del modernismo es omnipresente en este edificio de Domènech i Montaner. Aquí vemos un conjunto de motivos florales geométricos en las columnas de la terraza que rodea la sala Lluís Millet.

Colonnade in the Palau de la Música

The characteristic ornamentation of Modernist decoration is omnipresent in this building by Domènech i Montaner, such as the floral and geometrical motifs on the colonnade of the balcony encircling the Lluís Millet room.

Säulengang im Palau de la Música

Die Jugendstil-Ornamente sind allgegenwärtig in diesem Gebäude von Domènech i Montaner. Hier zum Beispiel sieht man geometrische Blumenmotive auf den Säulen der Terrasse, die den Saal Lluís Millet umgibt.

52 Palau de la Música Catalana

La fachada del Palau de la Música alcanza una fuerza expresiva y simbólica abrumadora, fruto de una concepción que integra arquitectura, escultura y artes decorativas. La reforma y ampliación se realizan según el proyecto del arquitecto Óscar Tusquets.

Palau de la Música Catalana

The façade of the Palau de la Música reaches overwhelming expressive and symbolic heights, the result of a concept that combines architecture, sculpture and the decorative arts. The reforms and extension are carrying out according to the project of the architect Óscar Tusquets.

Palau de la Música Catalana

Die überwältigende Ausdruckskraft und Symbolik der Fassade des Palau de la Música ist Ergebnis eines Konzeptes, das Architektur, Skulptur und die dekorativen Künste miteinander vereint. Die vor kurzem durchgeführte Renovierung und Erweiterung richtete sich nach einem Entwurf Óscar Tusquets.

53 Rincón del Eixample

La arquitectura modernista irrumpe en cualquier rincón del Eixample, como en esta perspectiva de la Diagonal dominada por el edificio neogótico de Puig i Cadafalch, la casa Terrades, popularmente denominada de "les Punxes".

Corner of the Eixample

Modernist architecture explodes on any corner of the Eixample district, as shown by this view of the Diagonal dominated by the neo-gothic building by Puig i Cadafalch, the Casa Terrades, Popularly known as "les Punxes".

Ein Winkel der Eixample

Die modernistische Architektur ist überall in dem Stadtteil Eixample präsent. Ein Beispiel dafür ist dieser Straßenabschnitt der Diagonal, der von dem neogotischen Gebäude von Puig i Cadafalch, der Casa Terrades, beherrscht wird, das im Volksmund „Les Punxes" genannt wird.

54 Escudo del mercado de la Boqueria

El mercado centenario de Sant Josep, llamado popularmente la Boqueria, muestra su escudo como un estandarte de su recinto de hierro, paraíso de gastrónomos.

Coat of arms of La Boqueria Market

The hundred-year-old Sant Josep's market, popularly known as La Boqueria, shows its coat of arms as a standard of the iron structure that encloses a gourmet's paradise.

Wappen der Markthalle La Boqueria

An der Fassade seiner eisernen Hallenkonstruktion kann der Besucher das Wappen des hundertjährigen Mercat de Sant Josep betrachten, ein Paradies für Feinschmecker, das im Volksmund La Boqueria genannt wird.

55 Vidriera de la Casa Lleó Morera

La extraordinaria vidriera semicircular del antiguo comedor de la Casa Lleó Morera, en el Passeig de Gràcia, destaca por su originalidad técnica y formal. Sus autores fueron el pintor Josep Pey y los vidrieros Joan Rigalt y Jeroni Granell.

Stained-glass of the Casa Lleó Morera

The semicircular stained-glass window of what was once the dining room of the Casa Lleó Morera, in Passeig de Gràcia, is extraordinary for both its technical and formal originality. It was the work of the painter Josep Pey and the glaziers Joan Rigalt and Jeroni Granell.

Mosaikfenster der Casa Lleó Morera

Das außergewöhnliche, halbrunde Mosaikfenster im ehemaligen Speisesaal des Hauses Lleó Morera am Passeig de Gràcia beeindruckt durch seine technische und konzeptuelle Originalität. Es wurde von dem Maler Josep Pey und den Kunstglasern Joan Rigalt und Jeroni Granell geschaffen.

56 "La Pedrera", de Gaudí

Llamada popularmente "La Pedrera", la monumental casa Milà combina en su fachada la abstracción de su masa de piedra ondulante con las formas barrocas de hierro forjado de los balcones.

"La Pedrera", by Gaudí

Popularly known as "La Pedrera", the façade of the monumental Casa Milà combines the abstraction of its mass of undulating stone with the Baroque shapes of the wrought iron balconies.

„La Pedrera", von Gaudí

Das im Volksmund als „La Pedrera" (Steinbruch) genannte Haus Casa Milà vereint in seiner Fassade die Abstraktion wogender Steinmassen mit den barocken Formen der schmiedeeisernen Balkongitter.

57 Balcón-tribuna de la casa Milà

El desarrollo de la fachada de la casa Milà resume una buena parte de la originalidad y conceptos constructivos y estéticos de la evolución de Gaudí. La contundencia de la piedra no está aquí exenta de ritmo y armonía.

Balcony-gallery of the Casa Milà

Tha façade of the Casa Milà synthesises the originality of Gaudí's concept of architecture and his aesthetic development. The force of the stone is not lacking in rhythm and harmony.

Emporenbalkon der Casa Milà

Die Fassade der Casa Milà spiegelt in hohem Maße Gaudís Originalität und seine baulichen und ästhetischen Konzepte wider. Die Wucht der steinernen Massen geht mit Harmonie und Rhythmus einher.

58 Terraza escalonada de la casa Milà

La absoluta originalidad constructiva de "La Pedrera" se desarrolla desde el sótano hasta la azotea, donde podemos observar algunos detalles de interés, como la situación de las buhardillas bajo el suelo escalonado de la terraza y la colocación de las enigmáticas chimeneas.

Terraced rooftop of the Casa Milà

The originality of the design of "La Pedrera" is constant throughout the building from the basement to the roof, where there are interesting details such as the garret windows below the terraced rooftop and the enigmatic chimney stacks.

Dachterrasse, Casa Milà

Die architektonische Einzigartigkeit der Casa Milà reicht vom Keller bis zur Dachterrasse voller interessanter Details wie zum Beispiel die unter den Stufen der Terrasse befindlichen Mansardenräume oder die Art und Weise, wie die merkwürdigen Schornsteine platziert sind.

59 Casa Batlló

Obra ya de plenitud, la casa Batlló anuncia "La Pedrera" con sus formas ondulantes y la disposición de balcones y tribunas. La decoración polícroma de la fachada tiene su culminación en la original resolución del tejado.

Casa Batlló

The undulating forms and the layout of the balconies and galleries on the Casa Batlló, an abundant work, give an indication of what was to come with "La Pedrera". The polychromatic decoration on the façade culminates in the highly original solution of the roof.

Casa Batlló

Die aus der Reifezeit Gaudís stammende Casa Batlló Rießin ihren geschwungenen Formen und der Anordnung der Balkone und Emporen bereits das nächste Meisterwerk „La Pedrera" erahnen. Die bunte Dekoration der Fassade wurde noch durch das originelle Dach unterstrichen.

60 Chimeneas de la casa Batlló

El grupo de chimeneas polícromas de la casa Batlló, es un detalle más de la importancia concedida por el arquitecto a la parte superior del edificio.

Chimneys on the Casa Batlló

The group of polychrome chimneys on the Casa Batlló is a mark of the importance Gaudí gave to the upper part of the building.

Schornsteine der Casa Batlló

Diese farbenprächtige Schornsteingruppe auf der Casa Batlló, die dem Betrachter der Fassade verborgen bleibt, ist ein weiterer Hinweis darauf, dass der Architekt dem oberen Teil des Gebäudes große Bedeutung beimaß.

61 Interior de la casa Batlló

La escalera de honor de la casa Batlló, en madera de roble y con desarrollo curvo, conducía al recibidor de la planta noble del edificio, situada en el primer piso.

Interior of the Casa Batlló

The main stairway of the Casa Batlló, in curving oak, led to the reception of the building's main floor, on the first floor.

Interieur der Casa Batlló

Die aus Eichenholz gefertigte, in Kurven verlaufende Prachttreppe der Casa Batlló führte zum Empfangssaal des edlen Stockwerkes in der ersten Etage des Gebäudes.

62 Casa Amatller

La inspiración neogótica domina la ejecución de la casa Amatller, obra de Puig i Cadafalch, en cuya parte superior se utilizó cerámica polícroma para adornar el remate escalonado.

Casa Amatller

Neo-gothic inspiration dominates the realisation of the Casa Amatller, a work by Puig i Cadafalch, polychrome ceramics being employed for the upper part to adorn the staggered top.

Casa Amatller

Neugotische Einflüsse dominierten bei der Gestaltung der Casa Amatller von Puig i Cadafalch. Für die Dekoration des Stufengiebels verwendete man farbige Keramik.

63 Detalles modernistas

El modernismo catalán supuso el florecimiento de las artes aplicadas y de las técnicas artesanales. En todos los proyectos arquitectónicos tenían cabida las realizaciones de ebanistería, forja, vidriería, cerámica, etc.

Modernist details

Applied arts and handicrafts flourished during the Catalan Modernist period. All architectural projects gave space to cabinet-making, wrought ironwork, glazing, ceramics, etc.

Jugendstil-Details

Der katalanische Jugendstil war die Blütezeit der angewandten Künste und handwerklichen Fähigkeiten. Die Kunsttischlerei, Goldschmiedearbeiten, Kunstglaserei, Kunstkeramik etc. spielten bei allen Architekturprojekten eine Rolle.

64 Arco de Triunfo

El Arco de Triunfo, situado en la parte baja del Passeig de Sant Joan, fue ideado por Josep Vilaseca como puerta de acceso monumental a la Exposición Universal de 1888, celebrada en el recinto del Parc de la Ciutadella.
La utilización del ladrillo visto se inspira en la arquitectura mudéjar.

Triumphal Arch

The Triumphal arch, situated at the lower end of Passeig Sant Joan, was designed by Josep Vilaseca as the gateway to the Universal Exhibition of 1888 held in Parc de la Ciutadella. The brick façade is influenced by Mudejar architecture.

Der Triumphbogen

Der Arc de Triomf im unteren Teil des Passeig de Sant Joan wurde von Josep Vilaseca als monumentales Zugangstor für die Weltausstellung von 1888 entworfen, die auf dem Gelände des Parc de la Ciutadella stattfand. Das Ziersteinmauerwerk ist vom Mudejar-Stil inspiriert.

65 Panorámica aérea de la Sagrada Familia

El templo de la Sagrada Familia, en su enclave del Eixample, es símbolo inconfundible de Barcelona en todo el mundo. A su ejecución dedicó Antoni Gaudí la mayor parte de su vida, sin poder culminarlo.

Aerial view of the Sagrada Família

The Temple of the Sagrada Família, located in the Eixample district, is the unmistakable symbol of Barcelona across the world. Antoni Gaudí devoted most of his life's work to the project, but was unable to see it completed.

Luftaufnahme der Sagrada Família

Die im Eixample gelegene Tempelkirche Sagrada Família gilt in der ganzen Welt als unverwechselbares Wahrzeichen Barcelonas. Antoni Gaudí widmete ihr den größten Teil seines Lebens, ohne sie jedoch vollenden zu können.

66 Detalle de la fachada del Nacimiento

De las tres fachadas de que dispondrá el templo de la Sagrada Familia, ésta es la única en la que Gaudí trabajó directamente. Destaca la exuberante ornamentación naturalista, con grupos escultóricos, animales, plantas, y otros elementos de simbología cristiana.

Detail of the Nativity façade

Of the three façades that will form the completed Sagrada Família, this is the only one to be finished in Gaudí's lifetime. Of special mention is the lush naturalist ornamentation, with sculptures, animals, plants and other elements with Christian symbolism.

Nahaufnahme der Geburtsfassade

Von den drei geplanten Fassaden der Sagrada Família sah Gaudí nur diese, die Christi Geburt zeigt, im vollendeten Zustand. Besonders auffallend ist die üppige naturalistische Ornamentierung mit Skulpturengruppen von Tieren, Pflanzen und anderen Elementen christlicher Symbolik.

67 Puente entre dos torres

Acceder a los interiores de la fachada del Nacimiento facilita un contacto más directo y emotivo con esta realización capital de Gaudí, resumen de todo su talento arquitectónico.

Bridge between two spires

Going inside the Nativity façade provides a more direct and emotive contact with Gaudí's masterpiece, the summary of all his architectural genius.

Brücke zwischen zwei Seitentürmen

Der Besuch der Geburtsfassade erlaubt einen direkten und aufregenden Zugang zu Gaudís Meisterwerk, das die Essenz seiner architektonischen Arbeit in sich birgt.

68 Detalles de la Sagrada Familia

La rica variedad de detalles del conjunto de la Sagrada Familia se nos ofrece al igual que un juego de descubrimientos, como este detalle de la fachada del Nacimiento, la escalera helicoidal del interior de una torre, la ornamentación de uno de los pináculos o el relieve de la clave de la cripta.

Details of the Sagrada Família

The rich assortment of details of the Sagrada Família is like a veritable treasure trove of discoveries, such as this detail of the Nativity façade, the helicoid stairway inside a spire, the ornamentation of one of the pinnacles or the relief on the crypt keystone.

Details der Sagrada Família

Die zahlreichen Details des Komplexes der Sagrada Família laden zu Entdeckungen ein. Hier sehen wir ein Detail an der Geburtsfassade, die spiralförmige Treppe im Inneren eines Turmes, die Verzierung eines der Giebel oder das Relief auf dem Schlussstein der Krypta.

69 Interior de la Sagrada Familia

La culminación del interior del templo se hace cada vez más patente a medida que se van completando las espectaculares columnas estriadas y ramificadas, de clara inspiración arbórea.

Interior of the Sagrada Família

The culmination of the inside of the temple becomes ever clearer as the spectacular stretching and ramified columns reach the top, with their obvious arboreal inspiration.

Innenraum der Sagrada Família

Die vollendete Schönheit des Inneren des Tempels wird immer deutlicher, je weiter die auffallenden, kannelierten und sich verzweigenden, von Bäumen inspirierten Säulen vervollständigt werden.

70 Fachada de la Pasión

La ejecución de los grupos escultóricos de la fachada de la Pasión, que ilustran los últimos días de la vida de Cristo, fueron encomendados al escultor catalán Josep Maria Subirachs.

Façade of the Passion

The completion of the sculptural groups on the façade of the Passion, which illustrate the last days of Christ's life, were entrusted to the Catalan sculptor Josep Maria Subirachs.

Die Passionsfassade

Die Skulpturengruppen der Passionsfassade, welche die letzten Tage im Leben Christus darstellen, sind ein Werk des katalanischen Bildhauers Josep Maria Subirachs.

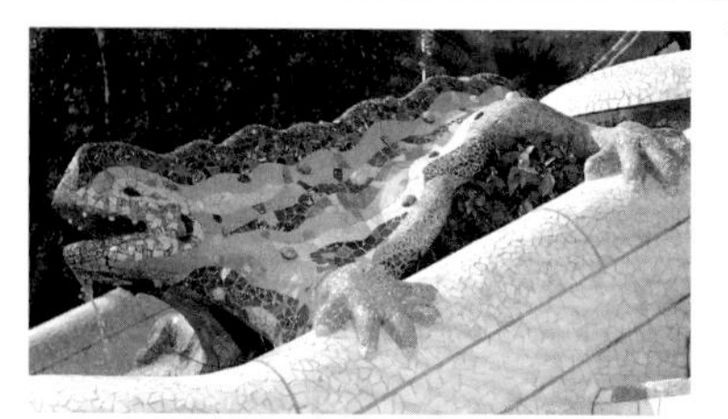

71 Dragón de la escalinata del Park Güell

El dragón situado en la doble escalinata de acceso al Park Güell se ha convertido en uno de los símbolos del parque; la interpretación mitológica lo convierte en el protector de las aguas subterráneas.

Dragon on the stairway of Park Güell

The dragon decorating the double stairway at the main entrance to Park Güell has become one of the park's identifying symbols. It represents the mythological guardian of the subterranean waters.

Die Drachenskulptur im Park Güell

Der an der doppelten Freitreppe zum Park Güell postierte Drache ist eines der Wahrzeichen des Parks. Der Mythologie zufolge ist er der Beschützer der Grundwasservorräte.

72 Un parque protegido por la UNESCO

Eusebi Güell encargó a Gaudí un proyecto de ciudad-jardín residencial influido por las ideas de los reformadores sociales ingleses de finales del siglo XIX. Las obras se desarrollaron entre 1900 y 1914. En 1984 fue declarado Patrimonio de la Humanidad por la UNESCO.

A park protected by UNESCO

Eusebi Güell, influenced by the ideology of English social reformers, commissioned Gaudí to create a project for a residential garden city. The work was carried out between 1900 and 1914, and in 1984 it was declared a World Heritage Site by UNESCO.

Ein von der UNESCO geschützter Park

Gaudí wurde von Eusebi Güell mit dem Projekt einer Gartenstadt beauftragt, das von den Ideen der englischen Sozialreformer beeinflusst war. Das Projekt wurde in den Jahren von 1900 bis 1915 durchgeführt. Im Jahre 1984 erklärte die UNESCO den Park zum Weltkulturerbe.

73 Banco de la plaza del Park Güell

Habitualmente, el público llena de vida y bullicio el banco ondulado que delimita la gran plaza-mirador del Park Güell. Su sección, obtenida del perfil ergonómico de un individuo sentado, y la disposición en meandros hacen que resulte idóneo para acoger la típica tertulia mediterránea.

Serpentine bench in Park Güell

The undulating bench that marks the boundary of the open square-panoramic viewpoint is usually full of the hurly-burly of life. Its layout, obtained from the profile of a person sitting down and the meandering semicircular recesses, make it the perfect spot for the typical Mediterranean pastime of sitting around chatting.

Bank des Platzes im Park Güell

Die gewundene Bank um den großen Platz des Park Güell zieht alle Besucher magnetisch an. Die ergonomische Form, die sich an der menschlichen Sitzhaltung orientiert, und die zahlreichen Windungen machen sie zu einem idealen Ort für die im Mittelmeerraum so beliebten Plauderstündchen.

74 Galería porticada del Park Güell

Las columnas inclinadas y el muro de contención de la galería porticada siguen la pendiente natural del terreno y se enlazan formando una bóveda de cañón.

Porched arcade in Park Güell

The oblique columns and retaining walls of the long arcade follow the natural slope of the land and form a barrel vault where they meet.

Säulengang im Park Güell

Die geneigten Säulen und die Stützmauer der langen Säulengalerie passen sich dem natürlichen Gefälle des Geländes an und formen zusammen ein Tonnengewölbe.

75 Pabellón del Park Güell

El pabellón de servicios del Park Güell, situado en la entrada, tiene una cúpula de tonos claros que contrasta con la piedra ocre de los muros. Un mirador circular con barandilla almenada corona la parte superior de la cúpula.

Pavilion in Park Güell

The lodge pavilion in Park Güell, located at the entrance, has a dome in light shades that contrasts with the ochre stone of the walls. A circular viewpoint with a crenelated rail crowns the upper part of the dome.

Pavillon im Park Güell

Die hellen Töne der Kuppel des Verwaltungsgebäudes im Park Güell kontrastieren mit dem ockerfarbenen Mauerwerk. Der obere Teil der Kuppel wird durch einen von Zinnen umgebenen Rundgang abgeschlossen.

76 Jardines del Park Güell

El Park Güell es la obra urbanística más completa y representativa de Gaudí, la aportación más específica al desarrollo modernista, con un distanciamiento evidente de las referencias a los estilos históricos. En su conjunto, destaca la armonización entre los elementos geológicos y vegetales.

Gardens in Park Güell

This is the most complete and representative of all Gaudí's planning projects. The movement away from past styles is obvious in this work, his most specific contribution to the development of Modernism. The harmony achieved between stonework and vegetation is particularly outstanding.

Gartenanlagen im Park Güell

Der Park Güell ist das repräsentativste städtebauliche Werk Gaudís, mit dem er sich deutlich von der historischen Architektur distanziert. Es gelang dem Künstler-Architekten hier, eine besondere Harmonie zwischen geologischen und pflanzlichen Elementen zu schaffen.

77 Columnata dórica. Park Güell

Las 86 columnas dóricas sostienen una parte de la gran plaza superpuesta. El espacio estaba destinado a mercado de la urbanización. El mosaico vidriado que reviste el techo alterna con plafones y motivos decorativos polícromos, proyectados por J.Mª Jujol, según directrices de Gaudí.

Doric colonnade in Park Güell

This hall of eighty-six Doric columns supporting part of the upper square was destined to be used as the marketplace. The glass mosaic covering the ceiling alternates with polychrome decorative ceiling roses and motifs designed by the architect Jujol, following Gaudí's guidelines.

Dorische Säulengruppe im Park Güell

Sechsundachtzig geneigte, dorische Säulen stützen einen Teil des großen Platzes; dieser Raum war als Markthalle der Gartenstadt gedacht. Das weißglasierte Deckenmosaik umsäumt Leuchten und vielfarbige Ornamente, die nach Gaudís Anweisungen vom Architekten Jujol entworfen wurden.

78 Casa Vicens

La casa que Gaudí construyó para el ceramista Manuel Vicens en 1878 se considera su primera obra importante; destaca por su concepción volumétrica, el empleo de los materiales y la policromía del revestimiento cerámico.

Casa Vicens

The house Gaudí built for the ceramist Manuel Vicens in 1878 is considered as his first major work. It stands out for its volumetric conception, the use of materials and the colouring of the ceramic-tiled decoration.

Casa Vicens

Gaudí erbaute dieses Haus, das als sein erstes wichtiges Werk angesehen wird, im Jahr 1878 für den Keramikfabrikanten Vicens. Besonders auffallend ist das volumetrische Konzept, die Verwendung der Materialien und die Vielfarbigkeit der Keramikverkleidung.

79 Museu de Zoologia desde el invernáculo

Entre los edificios singulares que hay en el Parc de la Ciutadella se encuentra el invernáculo, obra de Josep Amargós, y el que hoy es sede del Museu de Zoologia, realizado por Doménech i Montaner como café-restaurante para la Exposición de 1888.

The Museum of Zoology from the greenhouse

Among the unique buildings in Parc de la Ciutadella is the greenhouse, a work by Josep Amargós, today the headquarters of the Museum of Zoology, undertaken by Doménech i Montaner as a café-restaurant for the Exhibition of 1888.

Museu de Zoologia, Gewächshaus

Eines der einzigartigen Gebäude im Park de la Ciutadella ist das Gewächshaus von Josep Amargós. Ebenso bemerkenswert ist das Gebäude, in dem sich das Museu de Zoologia befindet, erbaut von Doménech i Montaner als Café-Restaurant für die Ausstellung 1888.

80 Detalle de la Casa Amatller

Entre las referencias neogóticas utilizadas en la Casa Amatller figura este relieve mitológico de Sant Jordi, esculpido por Eusebi Arnau.

Detail of the Casa Amatller

Among the neo-gothic references used in the Casa Amatller feature this mythological relief of St. George, sculpted by Eusebi Arnau.

Detail der Casa Amatller

Unter den neugotischen Motiven in der Casa Amatller findet sich dieses Relief des Heiligen Georg, ein Werk des Bildhauers Eusebi Arnau.

81 Interior del Palau Macaia

En este detalle del patio interior del Palau Macaia, obra de Puig i Cadafalch situada en el Passeig de Sant Joan, resaltan la ornamentación con relieve floral de la escalera y el trabajo de forja de la verja, tan representativos del modernismo.

Interior of the Palau Macaia

The detail of the inner courtyard of Puig i Cadafalch's Palau Macaia in Passeig de Sant Joan clearly shows the floral relief on the stairway and wrought ironwork of the gate, so typical of the Modernist period.

Interieur des Palau Macaia

Diese Nahaufnahme aus dem Innenhof des Palau Macaia, Werk des Architekten Puig i Cadafalch am Passeig de Sant Joan, zeigt zwei typische Jugendstilelemente in ihrer höchsten Vollendung, das Blumenrelief des Treppenornaments und die Schmiedearbeit am Gitter.

82 La escalera de la casa Manuel Felip

Son innumerables los detalles de construcción y ornamentación modernistas que se distribuyen por todo el Eixample, como esta escalera realizada por el arquitecto Telm Fernández.

Stairway in the Casa Manuel Felip

Countless attractive and interesting details of Modernist construction and ornamentation appeared throughout the entire Eixample district, such as this stairway by the architect Telm Fernández.

Treppe in der Casa Manuel Felip

Im Eixample lassen sich unzählige Details der Baukunst und Ausschmückungen des Modernismus entdecken, darunter diese Treppe des Architekten Telm Fernández.

83 La puerta del Dragón. Pavellons Güell

Inspirándose en el que guardaba la entrada del mitológico jardín de las Hespérides, Gaudí ideó este dragón de hierro forjado para la puerta principal de los Pavellons Güell. Su cuerpo reproduce la posición de las estrellas en las constelaciones de Dragón y Hércules.

The Dragon Gate at the Güell Pavillions

Inspired by the guardian of the mythological garden of the Hesperides, Gaudí designed this wrought iron dragon for the main entrance of the Güell Pavillions. Its form reproduces the position of the stars in the constellations of the Dragon and Hercules.

Drachentor, Pavellons Güell

Dieser ungewöhnliche, schmiedeeiserne Drachen wurde von Gaudí für das Haupttor der Pavellons Güell in Pedralbes in Anlehnung an den Garten der Hesperiden entworfen, dessen Tor von einem Drachen bewacht wurde. Sein Körper ist den Sternbildern Drache und Herkules nachempfunden.

84 Entrada a los Pavellons Güell

La entrada a la finca que la familia Güell poseía en el barrio de Pedralbes incluye este conjunto de edificaciones que flanquean la puerta del dragón, integrados por un pabellón de entrada, las caballerizas y un picadero.

Entrance to the Güell Pavillions

The entrance to the estate owned by the Güell family in the Pedralbes district includes this series of constructions that flank the Dragon Gate, composed of an entrance pavilion, the stables and a ring.

Eingang zu den Pavellons Güell

Die Einfahrt zum Gut der Familie Güell in dem Stadtteil Pedralbes wird von diesen Bauten begrenzt, welche das Drachentor säumen. Es handelt sich um einen Pavillon am Eingang, den Reitstall und eine Reitbahn.

85 Fachada posterior de la casa Comalat

La parte posterior de la casa Comalat, obra modernista de Salvador Valeri, presenta una solución bien diferente de su fachada principal. Aquí, las ondulantes galerías de madera y las ornamentaciones cerámicas parecen gozar de mayor libertad expresiva.

Rear façade of the Casa Comalat

The rear section of the Casa Comalat, a Modernist work by Salvador Valeri, provides a very distinct solution to that of the front part. Here, the undulating wooden galleries and the ceramic ornamentation seem to enjoy a greater level of expressive freedom.

Rückseite der Casa Comalat

Die Rückseite der Casa Comalat, eines Jugendstilgebäudes von Salvador Valeri, unterscheidet sich wesentlich von der Hauptfassade. Die gewölbten hölzernen Erker und die Keramikornamente scheinen von einer größeren gestalterischen Freiheit zu zeugen.

86 Interior de Bellesguard

La torre de Bellesguard, situada en la falda del Tibidabo, fue encargada a Gaudí en el año 1900.,
En su conjunto es de inspiración gótica, aquí vemos una parte del vestíbulo y de la escalera principal.

Interior of Bellesguard

The villa of Bellesguard, located at the foot of Tibidabo, was commissioned to Gaudí in 1900. It is a building inspired by Gothic architecture and here we see a part of the lobby and main stairway.

Interieur von Bellesguard

Das Landhaus Bellesguard am Fuße des Tibidabo wurde von Gaudí im Jahr 1900 errichtet. Das Bauwerk ist von der Gotik inspiriert, hier sehen wir einen Teil der Eingangshalle und der Haupttreppe.

87 Reja del Palau Güell

Este detalle de la parte superior de una de las puertas de entrada al palacio tiene un diseño de forja sinuoso con el que Gaudí se adelanta al que utilizará más tarde el modernismo.

Grille of the Palau Güell

This detail of the upper section of one of the palace's entrance doors has a sinuous wrought iron design with which Gaudí was ahead of his time in that this was used later by the Modernist movement.

Gitter des Palau Güell

Diese Details des oberen Teils einer der Eingangstüren des Palastes sind aus kurvenförmigen Schmiedeeisen, ein Element, das Gaudí später in seinen modernistischen Bauten verwenden würde.

88 Terraza del Palau Güell

La salida de humos y ventilaciones del palacio fueron tratadas por Gaudí de modo diverso, con ladrillo visto, revestimientos cerámicos de colores, losetas de mármol o piedras pequeñas.

Terrace of the Palau Güell

The smoke and ventilation outlets of the palace were dealt with by Gaudí in a different way, with brick façade, coloured ceramic tiling, marble floor tiles and small stones.

Terrasse des Palau Güell

Gaudí fand verschiedene Lösungen für den Rauchabzug und die Belüftung des Palastes, aus unverputztem Ziegelstein, mit Verkleidung aus bunter Keramik, Marmorfliesen oder kleinen Steinen.

89 Fundació Joan Miró. Montjuïc

Josep Lluís Sert realizó el proyecto arquitectónico que debía albergar la colección de obras donada por Joan Miró a la ciudad y que, al mismo tiempo, es sede del Centre d'Estudis d'Art Contemporani.

The Joan Miró Foundation. Montjuïc

Josep Lluís Sert undertook the architectural project that would house the collection and works donated by Joan Miró to the city and which is also the headquarters for the Study Center of Contemporany Art.

Fundació Joan Miró. Montjuïc

Der Entwurf für dieses Gebäude stammt von Josep Lluís Sert. Es beherbergt die Kunstsammlung, die Joan Miró der Stadt Barcelona stiftete, und ist zugleich Sitz des Centre d'Estudis d'Art Contemporani.

90 Interior de la Fundació Joan Miró

Hasta el momento, la Fundació Miró es uno de los museos más activos de la ciudad. Además de acoger la muestra permanente de la obra del artista, organiza de forma continuada numerosas exposiciones y actos culturales.

Interior of the Joan Miró Foundation

Until now, the Joan Miró Foundation has been one of the most active museums in the city. Apart from the permanent showing of the artist's work, the museum continuously puts on other exhibitions and cultural events.

Interieur der Fundació Joan Miró

Derzeit ist die Fundació Miró das aktivste Museum Barcelonas. Neben der ständigen Ausstellung der Werke Mirós finden laufend Ausstellungen anderer Künstler und weitere kulturelle Veranstaltungen statt.

91 Auditori Municipal

L'Auditori, obra del arquitecto Rafael Moneo, tiene una capacidad de 2.600 personas en la sala de conciertos sinfónicos, y de 700 en la de conciertos de cámara; dispone además de biblioteca, museo y un laboratorio de electroacústica, entre otros servicios y actividades.

The Municipal Auditorium

L'Auditori, work of the architect Rafael Moneo, has a capacity for 2.600 people in the concert hall and 700 in the chamber concert hall, as well as a library, museum and electro-acoustic laboratory, among other services and activities.

Auditori Municipal

L'Auditori, ist Werk des Architekten Rafael Moneo und hat Aufnahmekapazitäten für 2600 Personen im Saal für Symphoniekonzerte, für 700 Personen im Kammermusiksaal, und desweiteren gibt es eine Bibliothek, ein Museum und ein elektroakustisches Labor.

92 La ciudad a los pies del Tibidabo

Con la última luz de la tarde se encienden las primeras luces de la ciudad. A los pies de la montaña del Tibidabo, Barcelona es observada desde la atalaya del parque de atracciones. Por aquí ha pasado una buena parte de las alegrías infantiles de los barceloneses.

The city below Tibidabo

With the last rays of the evening sun, the first lights go on in the city. At the foot of the mountain of Tibidabo, Barcelona is seen from the watchtower of the amusement park. Many happy moments have been spent here by the children of Barcelona over the years.

Die Stadt am Fuße des Tibidabo

In der Abenddämmerung erglänzen die ersten Lichter der Stadt. Von einer Aussichtsplattform des Vergnügungsparks auf dem Tibidabo aus, der schon Generationen von Kindern erfreut hat, überblickt man das am Fuße des Berges liegende Barcelona.

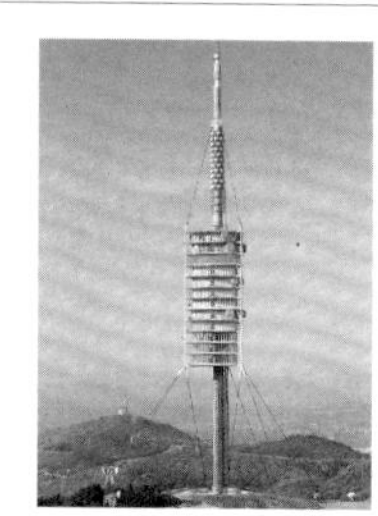

93 Torre de telecomunicaciones

Norman Foster es el autor de este moderno diseño para la nueva torre de telecomunicaciones que centraliza los servicios que utilizan esta tecnología. Se alza sobre la sierra de Collserola a 260 metros de altura.

Telecommunication tower

Norman Foster designed this modern telecommunication tower which centralises the services using this technology. It soars 260 metres above the Collserola hills.

Funkturm

Der 260 Meter hohe Funkturm, welcher der Verbesserung der Dienstleistungen im Kommunikationsbereich dient, befindet sich auf der Hügelkette Serra de Collserola. Der moderne Entwurf stammt von Norman Foster.

94 Bares y locales nocturnos

La vida nocturna ha experimentado un auge inusitado en estos últimos años. El protagonismo del diseño ha sido constante en la concepción de los nuevos locales que amenizan las noches de Barcelona.

Bars and nightspots

The city's nightlife has been thriving in recent years. Hi-tech design plays an important role in the conceptualisation of the new spots that liven up the Barcelona nights.

Bars und Nachtlokale

Barcelonas Nachtleben hat sich in den letzten Jahren stürmisch entwickelt. Modernes Design spielt bei der Einrichtung neuer Lokale eine wesentliche Rolle.

95 Casa Arnús. "El Pinar"

El modernismo, en su expresión ornamental más epidérmica, fue adaptado por corrientes más conservadoras y eclécticas; como en el caso del arquitecto Enric Sagnier, autor de este palacete de inspiración gótica que adquiere especial relevancia entre las sombras de la falda del Tibidabo.

Casa Arnús. "El Pinar"

Modernism, in its most superficial expression, was adopted by the more conservative and eclectic sections of society of the time. This mansion along neo-gothic lines, by the architect Enric Sagnier, is especially striking here among the shadowy slopes of Tibidabo.

Casa Arnús. „El Pinar"

Elemente des Modernismus in seiner reinsten Prägung wurden von anderen, etwas konservativeren Strömungen übernommen. Dieses Palais mit gotischen Anklängen, ein Werk des Architekten Sagnier, erhält durch die Schattenlage am Hang des Tibidabos zusätzliche Wirkung.

96 Anillo olímpico de Montjuïc

El entorno del anillo olímpico, con instalaciones deportivas como el Palau Sant Jordi y el renovado Estadio Olímpico, se ha convertido en una espectacular zona de ocio de gran importancia ciudadana.

The Olympic Area of Montjuïc

The presence of the new sporting venues, such as the Palau Sant Jordi and the refurbished Olympic Stadium, have been decisive in the spectacular urban development around the Olympic Area, making it an important leisure area for the people of Barcelona.

Der Olympiakomplex, Montjuïc

Die für die Olympiade errichteten und renovierten Sportanlagen auf dem Montjuïc wie der Palau Sant Jordi und das Olympiastadium sind heutzutage eine unentbehrliche Bereicherung für das Freizeitangebot der Stadt.

97 *Aurigas* de Pablo Gargallo

Los dos aurigas que ya figuraron en el viejo estadio de Montjuïc dominan ahora, desde lo alto de las puertas de entrada, la hermosa perspectiva sobre el Palau Sant Jordi y el resto del anillo olímpico.

Charioteers by Pablo Gargallo

The two charioteers that were present in the old Montjuïc stadium before its renovation now look out over the splendid sight of the Palau Sant Jordi and the rest of the Olympic Area.

Wagenlenker von Pablo Gargallo

Die beiden Wagenlenker, die schon im alten Stadium auf dem Montjuïc ihren Platz hatten, beherrschen jetzt vom Eingang des Stadiums aus das schöne Panorama mit dem Palau Sant Jordi und den anderen Olympia-Sportanlagen.

98 Teatre Nacional de Catalunya

El Teatre Nacional de Catalunya, obra de inspiración neoclásica del arquitecto Ricardo Bofill, situado junto a L'Auditori en la zona de Glòries dispone de dos salas para representaciones con una capacidad para 1.000 y 500 espectadores, respectivamente.

The National Theatre of Catalonia

The National Theatre of Catalonia, a work of neo-classical inspiration by the architect Ricardo Bofill, situated alongside L'Auditori in the Glòries area of the city, has two halls for performances with capacities for 1.000 and 500 spectators, respectively.

Teatre Nacional de Catalunya

Das Nationaltheater von Katalonien ist ein von der Neoklassik inspiriertes Werk des Architekten Ricardo Bofill in der Nähe L'Auditori am Platz Glòries.
Es gibt zwei Aufführungssäle mit einer Aufnahmekapazität für 1000 bzw. 500 Zuschauer.

99 Escultura de Georg Kolbe

En 1985 se reconstruyó el pabellón de Alemania de la Exposición Internacional de 1929, obra de Mies van der Rohe, con los mismos materiales y mobiliario originales. En su patio interior figura una réplica en bronce de la escultura de Georg Kolbe *Morgen* (La mañana).

Sculpture by Georg Kolbe

The German Hall by Mies van der Rohe for the 1929 Barcelona International Exhibition was rebuilt in 1985 on the same site, using the original construction materials and furnishings. The inner courtyard features a bronze replica of the sculpture by Georg Kolbe, *Morgen* (Morning).

Skulptur von Georg Kolbe

Der von Mies van der Rohe als deutscher Beitrag zur Weltausstellung entworfene Pavillon wurde 1985 mit dem Baumaterial und Mobiliar des Originals rekonstruiert. Im Innenhof des Gebäudes findet sich eine Reproduktion der Skulptur *Morgen* von Georg Kolbe.

100 Mamut del Parc de la Ciutadella

Son numerosos los rincones evocadores distribuidos por el Parc de la Ciutadella, como este dominio del prehistórico mamut que encontramos junto al lago.

Mammoth in Parc de la Ciutadella

There are many evocative corners strewn around Parc de la Ciutadella, such as this prehistoric mammoth that overlooks the lake.

Das Mammut im Parc de la Ciutadella

Eines der interessanten Details im Parc de la Ciutadella ist diese Statue eines prähistorischen Mammuts in Originalgröße.

101 Parc del Laberint

El laberinto forma parte de una antigua finca con edificaciones neoclásicas –hoy parque público– situada junto al velódromo de Horta. En la zona central de sus amplios jardines se encuentra el mitológico recinto.

Parc del Laberint

The maze forms part of an old estate with neo-classical buildings – today a public park – situated alongside the Horta Velodrome. The maze is situated in the heart of these spacious gardens.

Parc del Laberint

Das Labyrinth neben dem Velòdrom d'Horta, einer modernen Radrennbahn, gehörte ursprünglich zu einem Grundstück mit klassizistischen Bauten, das heute ein öffentlicher Park ist. Die mythologische Anlage liegt im Zentrum der ausgedehnten Gärten.

102 Puente de Bac de Roda

El puente-escultura del arquitecto e ingeniero Santiago Calatrava, simboliza la nueva realidad viaria de Barcelona, enlaza los sectores norte y sur de los barrios de levante de la ciudad.

Bac de Roda Bridge

This bridge-sculpture, by the engineer and architect Santiago Calatrava, symbolises city's new road network and joins the northern and southern districts of the Barcelona's eastern area.

Die Brücke Bac de Roda

Die von dem Ingenieur Santiago Calatrava entworfene Brücke verbindet im Osten Barcelonas die südlichen mit den nördlichen Vierteln. Die Brücke ist ein Symbol für die modernen Verkehrsbauten der Stadt.

103 Parc de l'Espanya Industrial

Concebido como unas modernas termas romanas, el parque se inscribe dentro de la más pura tradición mediterránea. En torno al agua, la vegetación y las gradas acogen al paseante y le ofrecen la calma y el sosiego en una zona densamente poblada.

Parc de l'Espanya Industrial

Conceived along the lines of a modern Roman spa, the park has been designed within the framework of pure Mediterranean traditions. Around the water, the vegetation and the tiers of steps offer an oasis of peace and quiet in the heart of a densely populated district.

Parc de l'Espanya Industrial

Modernen römischen Thermen gleich setzt dieser Park althergebrachte mediterrane Traditionen fort. Die Grünanlagen und Tribünen rund um das Wasser bieten dem Besucher mitten in einem dichtbesiedelten Stadtteil die Möglichkeit zur Ruhe und Entspannung.

104 Interior del Aquàrium

Las instalaciones del Aquàrium ofrecen un espectáculo insólito en todas su dependencias, pero nada comparable a la proximidad que sentimos en el túnel transparente de observación con los tiburones.

Interior of the Aquàrium

The Aquarium provides a stunning spectacle in all its sections, but nothing can be compared to the closeness we feel to the sharks in the transparent observation tunnel.

Im Aquàrium

Alle Teile des Aquariums bieten dem Besucher ein einzigartiges Schauspiel, aber keines davon ist so beeindruckend wie die Nähe, die man im transparenten Tunnel zu den Haifischen verspürt.

105 Aquàrium

Instalado en la nueva área del Maremàgnum, el Aquàrium es uno más de los numerosos reclamos lúdicos que ofrece la nueva fachada marítima de la ciudad.

Aquàrium

Situated in the new Maremàgnum area, the Aquarium is one of the most popular leisure spots on offer along the city's new seafront.

Aquàrium

Mitten im Maremàgnum gelegen ist das Aquàrium eine Attraktion mehr, die uns die jetzt zum Meer hin offene Stadt zu bieten hat.

106 Palau Sant Jordi

El Palau Sant Jordi, obra del arquitecto japonés Arata Isozaki, es la construcción más representativa entre las que configuran el anillo olímpico de Montjuïc. Su ejecución es producto de una compleja obra de ingeniería informatizada.

Palau Sant Jordi

The Palau Sant Jordi, work of the Japanese architect Arata Isozaki, is the most representative building that makes up the Montjuïc Olympic Area. Its construction is the result of a complex system of computerised engineering.

Palau Sant Jordi

Der Sportpalast des japanischen Architekten Arata Isozaki ist das repräsentativste Bauwerk des Olympiakomplexes auf dem Montjuïc. Er ist das Ergebnis der Kombination modernster Ingenieurtechnik mit computergestütztem Design.

107 Copito de Nieve, barcelonés ilustre

La popularidad de Copito de Nieve, único gorila albino del que se tiene noticia, supera los límites del Parque Zoológico, su residencia. Quizá no haya otro animal vivo tan emblemático como él.

Floquet de Neu, a citizen of Barcelona

The popularity of Floquet de Neu (Snowflake), the only known example of an albino gorilla, goes beyond the limits of the Zoo, his home. There is perhaps no other animal that is as emblematic as Snowflake.

Der berühmte Floquet de Neu

Floquet de Neu (Schneeflocke), der einzige bekannte Albino Gorilla, ist nicht nur in Barcelona eine Berühmtheit. Wohl kaum ein anderes lebendes Tier auf der Welt ist im gleichen Masse zum Wahrzeichen einer Stadt geworden.

108 Barrio de la Vila Olímpica

La concepción global de la Vila Olímpica se debió al equipo de arquitectos Martorell-Bohigas-Mackay-Puigdomènech, que transformaron una antigua zona industrial en un nuevo barrio residencial con la participación de más de veinticinco estudios de arquitectura.

The Vila Olímpica district

The global conception of the Olympic Village is the work of the architectural team of Martorell-Bohigas-Mackay-Puigdomènech, which transformed the old industrial area into a new residential district with the participation of over twenty-five architectural studios.

Viertel der Vila Olímpica

Der globale Entwurf der Olympiastadt stammt von dem Architektenteam Bohigas-Mackay-Puigdomènech, die aus einem ehemaligen Industriegebiet ein neues Wohnviertel gemacht haben. Bei diesem Projekt waren mehr als 25 Architekturstudios beteiligt.

109 Claustro del Monestir de Pedralbes

Muestra del mejor gótico catalán, el Monestir de Pedralbes, fundado en 1326, cuenta con este soberbio claustro cuadrado de tres galerías superpuestas. El recinto acoge también la colección Thyssen-Bornemisza, que ha enriquecido la oferta museística de la ciudad.

Cloister of the Monastery of Pedralbes

An example of the best of Catalan Gothic, the Monestir de Pedralbes, founded in 1326, has this superb cloister framed by three superimposed galleries. The site also houses the Thyssen-Bornemisza collection, enriching the city's artistic and cultural heritage.

Kreuzgang des Monestir de Pedralbes

Das Kloster von Pedralbes aus dem Jahre 1326 ist eines der besten Beispiele für die katalanische Gotik. Das Kloster besitzt einen wundervollen, quadratischen Kreuzgang mit drei Galerien und beherbergt außerdem die Sammlung Thyssen-Bornemisza, eine kulturelle Bereicherung für die Stadt.

110 *Elogio del agua*

El Parc de la Creueta del Coll es un claro ejemplo de actuación urbanística que incorpora la presencia de artistas de prestigio internacional, como este *Elogio del agua* del escultor vasco Eduardo Chillida.

In praise of water

The Parc de la Creueta del Coll is a clear example of urbanism that involves internationally famous artists, such as this *Elogi de l'aigua* (In praise of water) by the Basque sculptor Eduardo Chillida.

Lobpreisung des Wassers

Der Parc de la Creueta del Coll ist ein deutliches Beispiel für einen urbanistischen Eingriff, an dem international bekannte Künstler beteiligt waren. Hier befindet sich unter anderem das Werk *Elogi de l'aigua* (Lobpreisung des Wassers) des baskischen Bildhauers Eduardo Chillida.

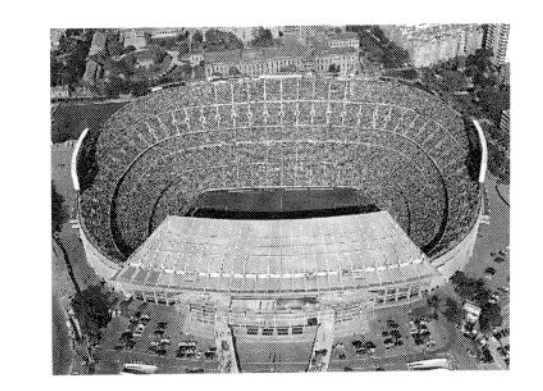

111 Estadio del Fútbol Club Barcelona

Situado en la parte alta de la Diagonal, el estadio del Nou Camp tiene un aforo de 98.000 espectadores y figura entre las mejores construcciones de arquitectura deportiva. Más de cien mil socios siguen con apasionamiento las actividades del club.

Barcelona Football Club Stadium

Situated in the high part of Diagonal, the Nou Camp stadium has a capacity for 98,000 spectators and features amongst the very best pieces of sports architecture. Over one hundred thousand members follow the club's progress passionately.

Stadium des Futbol Club Barcelona

Das im oberen Teil der Avinguda Diagonal gelegene Stadium Nou Camp hat eine Aufnahmekapazität für 98.000 Zuschauer. Es zählt zu den architektonisch gelungensten Sportstadien. Über hunderttausend Mitglieder verfolgen das Geschehen in diesem Klub.

112 Fuego y diablos

Las tradiciones populares se viven con intensidad a lo largo del año, especialmente las de la patrona de la ciudad, la virgen de la Mercè, en muchas de ellas se organizan "correfocs", como éste protagonizado por festivos diablos.

Fire and Devils

Popular traditions live on throughout the year, especially during the festival in honour of the city's patron saint, the virgin of the Mercè. In many of them "correfocs", running firework displays, are organised, such as this one being led by the festival devils.

Feuer und Teufel

Die volkstümlichen Traditionen werden das ganze Jahr über aufrecht erhalten, vor allem bei dem Fest zu Ehren der Schutzheiligen der Stadt, der Jungfrau „de la Mercè". Bei vielen dieser Feste wird ein „correfocs" wie dieser organisiert, bei dem die festlichen Teufel die Hauptrolle spielen.

113 Mosaico romano

El mosaico romano *Las tres Gracias* fue hallado en Barcelona y es una de las innumerables piezas arqueológicas del pasado histórico de la ciudad que se pueden admirar en el Museu Arqueològic de Montjuïc.

Roman mosaic

The Roman mosaic of the *Three Graces* was uncovered in Barcelona and is one of the countless archaeological pieces of the city's history that can be seen in the Museu Arqueològic de Montjuïc.

Römisches Mosaik

Das in Barcelona entdeckte, römische Mosaik *Tres Gràcies* ist eines der unzähligen archäologischen Stücke der historischen Vergangenheit der Stadt, die man im Museu Arqueològic de Montjuïc bewundern kann.

114 Pantocrátor románico

El Pantocrátor de la iglesia románica de Santa Maria de Taüll, se exhibe en el Museu Nacional d'Art de Catalunya, donde encontramos la mejor colección de pintura mural románica del mundo.

Romanesque Christ Pantocrator

The Pantocrator comes from the Romanesque church of Santa Maria de Taüll and is on show at the Museu Nacional d'Art de Catalunya, which houses the biggest collection of Romanesque mural painting in the world.

Römischer Pantokrator

Das Christusbild stammt aus der romanischen Kirche Santa Maria de Taüll und wird im Museu Nacional d'Art de Catalunya ausgestellt, in dem der Besucher die umfassendste Sammlung römischer Wandgemälde findet.

115 Fundació Antoni Tapies

La Fundació Antoni Tapies, prestigioso centro de actividad cultural, tiene su sede en este edificio de Domènech i Montaner, construcción pionera del modernismo catalán. La escultura *Núvol i cadira*, obra del propio Antoni Tapies, ocupa la parte superior del edificio.

The Antoni Tapies Foundation

The Antoni Tapies Foundation, a centre of intense cultural activity, occupies this building by Domènech i Montaner, considered at its time of construction to be a piece of pioneering Catalan Modernism. The sculpture *Núvol i Cadira* (Cloud and Chair), by Antoni Tapies himself, is situated on the roof of the building.

Fundació Antoni Tapies

Die Fundació Antoni Tapies, eine angesehene Kulturstiftung, hat ihren Sitz in einem der ersten Gebäude des katalanischen Modernismus, errichtet von Domènech und Montaner. Die Skulptur *Núvol i Cadira* (Wolke und Stuhl) von Tàpies nimmt den oberen Teil des Gebäudes ein.

116 Patio central del Museu Picasso

La sede del Museu Picasso se encuentra repartida entre varios palacios a lo largo de la calle de Montcada. La entrada principal es la del Palacio Berenguer Aguilar, originario del siglo XV.

Central courtyard of the Museu Picasso

The Picasso Museum is found spread through several palaces along Montcada Street, the main entrance being found in this Palau Berenguer Aguilar, dating from the 15th century.

Zentraler Innenhof des Museu Picasso

Der Sitz des Picasso-Museums verteilt sich über mehrere Paläste in der Straße Montcada, der Haupteingang ist im Palau Berenguer Aguilar, der aus dem 15. Jahrhundert stammt.

117 Panorama de la ciudad

La ciudad abierta al Mediterráneo es la imagen que mejor evoca la naturaleza de Barcelona. Entre el perfil protector de la sierra de Collserola y el mar, por el entramado vivo de calles y barrios, transcurre la vida de los barceloneses.

Panorama of the city

The city open to the Mediterranean is the image that best evokes the nature of Barcelona. Between the Collserola range and the sea, among the throbbing network of streets and neighbourhoods, the lives of Barcelona's inhabitants take place.

Panoramablick auf die Stadt

Barcelona als eine zum Meer hin offene Stadt, dieses Bild gibt den Charakter der Stadt am besten wieder. Zwischen der schützenden Hügelkette Sierra de Collserola und dem Meer verläuft das Leben der Einwohner in den lebendigen Straßen und Vierteln.

118 Cielos despejados en Catalunya

El suave clima mediterráneo hace que sea frecuente la mención del buen tiempo en Catalunya a través de la televisión autonómica TV3.

Clear skies over Catalonia

The mild Mediterranean climate allows TV3, the local television station, to frequently forecast good weather for Catalonia.

Wolkenloser Himmel über Katalonien

Das sanfte Mittelmeerklima sorgt dafür, dass beim autonomen katalanischen Fernsehsender TV3 oft von schönem Wetter in Katalonien die Sprache ist.

119 Casa Batlló

Toda la sutileza cromática de la casa Batlló, y especialmente las de las tejas colocadas como escamas, se pone de manifiesto con la iluminación nocturna del edificio.

Casa Batlló

The floodlit of the Casa Batlló reveals the full range and subtlety of its colour scheme, especially that of the roof tiles placed like scales.

Casa Batlló

Bei Nacht bringt die Beleuchtung der Fassade der Casa Batlló die Feinheiten ihrer Farbgebung erst richtig zur Geltung.

Edición / Published by / Verlag: Triangle Postals SL

Coordinación / Coordination / Koordination: Paz Marrodán / Jaume Serrat

Textos / Text / Texte: Borja Calzado

Translation / Übersetzung: Steve Cedar / Susanne Engler

Diseño gráfico / Design / Gestaltung: America Sanchez scp / Joan Colomer

Fotografías / Photography / Fotografien:
Pere Vivas
1, 3, 4, 5, 6, 7, 8, 9, 11, 12, 13, 14, 15, 16, 17, 19, 21, 22, 24, 25, 26, 28, 29, 30, 33, 34, 36, 37, 38, 40, 41, 42, 43, 44, 45, 46, 47, 48, 50, 51, 52, 54, 55, 56, 58, 62, 63a, 63b, 64, 66, 67, 68, 70, 72, 73, 74, 76, 77, 79, 80, 82, 83, 84, 85, 89, 91, 92, 93, 94, 95, 96, 99, 100, 101, 102, 106, 107, 108, 110, 115, 116, 118, 119
Juanjo Puente / Pere Vivas
69, 98, 104, 105
Ricard Pla
2, 18, 20, 31, 35, 39, 49, 53, 57, 60, 63c, 63d, 71, 75, 81, 90, 97, 103, 112
Ricard Pla / Pere Vivas
10, 59, 61, 78, 86, 87, 88
Lluís Bertrán
23, 27
Jordi Todó, Tavisa
65, 111, 117
MHCB. Museu d'Història de la Ciutat (Pere Vivas)
32, 109
Museu d'Arqueologia de Catalunya
113
MNAC. Museu Nacional d'Art de Catalunya (Calveras, Mèrida, Sagristà)
114

Impresión / Printed by / Druck: Indústries Gràfiques Viking, SA

Papel / Paper / Papier: Creator Silk, 150 gr/m². Torraspapel SA

Depósito legal: B-24.573-2001
ISBN: 84-8478-004-X

Triangle Postals:
Menorca
Tel. (34) 971 15 04 51 / Fax (34) 971 15 18 36
Barcelona
Tel (34) 93 218 77 37 / E-mail paz@teleline.es
www.trianglepostals.com